OVER THE HILL . . .
AND INTO THE WOODS!

OVER THE HILL . . .
AND INTO THE WOODS!

A Senior's Guide
to the Great Outdoors

HERB GORDON

THE DERRYDALE PRESS
Lanham and New York

THE DERRYDALE PRESS

Published in the United States of America
by The Derrydale Press
A Member of the Rowman & Littlefield Publishing Group
4501 Forbes Boulevard, Suite 200, Lanham, Maryland 20706

Distributed by NATIONAL BOOK NETWORK, INC.
First Derrydale Printing 2003
Copyright © 2003 by The Derrydale Press

Library of Congress Control Number: 2002117096
ISBN 1-58667-094-8 alk. paper

♾™ The paper used in this publication meets the minimum
requirements of American National Standard for Information
Sciences—Permanence of Paper for Printed Library Materials,
ANSI/NISO Z39.48–1992.
Manufactured in the United States of America.

Ah! fill the Cup:—what boots it to repeat
How Time is slipping underneath our Feet:
Unborn TO-MORROW, and dead YESTERDAY
Why fret about them if TO-DAY be sweet!

—Omar Khayyam, 11th-century
Persian mathematician and poet

CONTENTS

INTRODUCTION

Give me a young man in whom there is
something of the old, and an old man with
something of the young: guided so, a man may
grow old in body, but never in mind.

—Cicero, *De Senectute* (106–43 B.C.)

My first inclination was to reject one couple who
had applied to participate in a weeklong, national
Sierra Club canoe trip I would lead in the forested
wilderness of northern Quebec. I mean: This
was wilderness! For this particular trip on the
headwaters of the Ottawa river, we would paddle
about 90 miles, totally self-contained, with an average of one carry-everything-across portage
daily. We were unlikely to meet another person in
that wild country during the whole trip. One of
our endless tasks was simply to find enough clear
space ashore every night to make camp and pitch

five tents for the eight guests planned for the trip—whose usual age range was from their late 20s to 50-plus—plus myself and my co-leader, Scott. Scott is not only a superior paddler of both canoes and whitewater kayaks, but he is also my 33-year-old grandson.

The reason for my initial concern was an almost instinctive bias. Not based on color or religion, but because both were in their late seventies. They were the oldest paddlers who had ever applied for one of my annual wilderness trips. Were they really too old, though? Of course not. How could I even contemplate such a stupid thing without first familiarizing myself with their physical capacities? And interests? And experience?

After a careful review of their applications and personal interviews, they were signed up.

To my private pleasure, each turned out to be an excellent and sturdy paddler and camper. They handled two days of heavy rains and wind without problems or complaints. Ashore, they promptly and pleasantly did their full share of work on tasks assigned on a rotating duty roster. Their cheerful personalities served us all well. On several pleasant early mornings they were the first ones up, tossing fishhooks into the water to snag a delicious added tidbit for breakfast. What they caught and we didn't eat were released.

There is the inevitable moral to my story of how these 70-plus-year-olds paddled and fished and camped: Age is no real criterion for evaluating the physical and mental capacities of seniors, whether they are in their 60s or 90s, though in our "youth-is-everything" society, it often seems to be.

Being physically capable and emotionally qualified to tramp trails, paddle distant rivers, ski, or
simply pitch tents for a few days in a great national
wilderness region as we grow older is not only a
magnificent addition to our lifestyles but also is key
to the simple fact that *physical and mental activity*
are the basic elements for a healthy senior life.

The truly healthy 65- or 75- or 85-year-old
doesn't depend on nothing but a weird meat, a veg-
gie diet, or their parent's genes for a long, healthy
life. The two keys, again? *Physical and mental activity.*

Be dynamic! Whether you are newly retired or
have been drifting into a nothingness lifestyle,
don't float into an early departure. Put yourself into
the pleasure of staying involved—mentally and
physically.

Keep your mind involved. Read books. Become
a conservation activist. Study for another degree.
Argue over the merits of the play you saw last
night. Acquire a pup, a breed that needs an outdoor
walk several times a day, and learn from the SPCA
or a breeder how to train a four-footed friend properly. That will involve both physical and mental activities.

You haven't been active outdoors?

Toss out that old canvas shelter and buy a sleek
four-season bubble tent, and use it. Climb a mountain, or walk a trail. Travel the outdoors by foot or
canoe. Cross-country ski on the newly fallen snows,
join the 70+ Ski Club, or keep your knees busy on a
mountain bicycle.

Sit in front of your tent and relearn the con-
stellations in an area where the stars shine with

unaccustomed brilliance. Camp in the shelter of towering pines, or in a sagebrush valley. Enjoy the physical good health that is the beneficent gift of the outdoor experience, but not if your outdoor experience is only a daily walk from the car parked as close to the shopping mall as you can find a spot.

CHAPTER ONE

HEALTH AND SAFETY

Outdoor Trends

In a report on today's graying outdoor population, *AMC Outdoors*, the magazine of the Appalachian Mountain Club, says that "hikers aged 45 and over far outnumber those between the ages of 25 and 34." It estimates that there are 77 million or so baby boomers, "many of whom have identified with the wilderness since the 1960s when outdoor sports became popular."

By 2005, hiking, road biking, and perhaps even mountain biking will be dominated by middle-aged men and women, according to studies by the Sporting Goods Manufacturers' Association of America. Mike May, a spokesman for the association, says that in the past ten years "hundreds of companies that design packaged hiking and biking trips have sprung up to meet the rising demand from this middle-aged and older group."

The trend toward lighter products also is widespread in the sports manufacturing industries. As examples: The bicycle manufacturer, Trek, has introduced the R200, which lowers the impact on older cyclists' back and knees. Mountainsmith, which makes backpacks, has introduced a line of convertible packs easier for older people to use because they have a simpler and lighter design. Experts acknowledge that even though many outdoor products are lighter and easier to use than they once were, most manufacturers avoid the implication that they are for "older citizens."

Whether the trend of an increasing number of seniors either adopting or retaining a lifelong interest in the wilderness will continue is uncertain. Some authorities look at the growing interest among today's 17- to 35-year-olds in the Internet, computer games, and TV, and their decreasing interest in the physically active outdoor and wilderness activities of their parents, as an indication of a let's-do-less-physically tomorrow generation edging to take over—with their bigger, gaudier microparagadgetry.

Active and Healthy

The great end of life is not knowledge
but action.
—Thomas Huxley (1825–1895)

Even the idea that seniors should stay active as they grew older once was ridiculed as a quick way to an early death rather than as a stairway to a longer life. Among the first authorities on the elderly to recognize this as a myth was Dr. Bernice L. Neugarten, who proceeded to shatter traditional medical and popular folk views on the elderly in the early 1940s. She once wrote: "A set of stereotypes has grown up that older persons are sick, poor, enfeebled, isolated and desolated." Arguing against such ideas, she pointed to a steadily declining retirement age after World War II and said that people 55 and older were quitting work to seek more healthful and more active lives.

In a major article on old age in March 2001, the *New York Times* noted the widespread use of medication and psychiatric help to bring relief to the emotional ills of the aging, but it also asked: Can you change in older age? Experts say that people who are used to asking questions and solving problems can keep it up forever—if they are motivated: "'There is increasing data showing that the more people remain active, physically and mentally, the better they will continue to function,' said Dr. Philip V. Jeste, director of geriatric psychiatry at the University of California, San Diego."

Dr. Zira DeFries, an 83-year-old psychiatrist, highlighted a significant reason for why this book you now are reading, which guides seniors into outdoor activities, was written when she was quoted as saying: "Formerly old folks were very passive. Now that ageism is no longer politically correct, we're beginning to stick up for our rights and activities. [I applaud that.] It's very good for our mental health."

If you need to change your life to include the wilderness do so! If you have been an outdoorswoman or man all your life, age is no reason to give up a clear sky or a quiet valley, or challenging a mountain with a backpack—or camera. Yes, there is a major time factor in devouring the magnificent pleasure of the outdoors. Start now. Tomorrow may be too late.

The woods await!

There is an eternal magnificence in the still untamed backcountry. It remains as compelling for veterans of wood, fire, and tent, who have known its spiritual awe all their lives, as it instantly becomes for those newly arrived in the ranks of retired seniors who welcome the exalted opportunity of sleeping in a tent they erected with their own weary hands.

When Henry David Thoreau moved beyond the city into the then-remote wilds of the New England mountains, he wrote: "I went to the woods because I wished to live deliberately, to front only the essential facts of life, and see if I could not learn what it had to teach, and not, when I came to die, discover I had not lived."

John Muir, whose love of the distant trees and untouched peaks led to the creation of the Sierra Club, found it "hard to realize that every camp of (women and) men or beast has this glorious starry firmament for a roof! In such places, standing alone on the mountain top it is easy to realize that whatever special nests we make—leaves and moss like the marmots and birds, or tents or piled stone—we all dwell in a house of one room—the world with the firmament for its roof—and are sailing the celestial spaces without leaving any track."

For those who have not yet found this inner glory, may you be tempted into the wilderness by the words of "The Old Woodsman": "We do not go to the green woods and crystal waters to rough it, we go to smooth it. We get it rough enough at home." The Old Woodsman was George Sears, the author of *Woodcraft,* who wrote under his Indian name, Nessmuk. Published in the late 1880s, *Woodcraft* was the first guide to lightweight, conservation-oriented camping, canoeing, hunting, and fishing in America.

But there is far more to this book than poeticizing the wilds or citing the healthy aspects of backpacking the wilderness. It is filled with practical advice and guidance for seniors on every aspect of enjoying the back country—from hiking boots to the latest in self-supporting tents, and from a refresher course on map reading to how to use a GPS to locate yourself. Add new flavors to healthy, lightweight camp recipes and learn how to figure meal quantities for long outdoor travel. Read about modern wilderness clothing and camp gear, then go buy what you need to return to the outdoors. Here also are special physical exercises for specific problems that seniors encounter. And so much more.

When we're young, we know all the answers. Only as we step into tomorrow do we realize that in those days we didn't even know all of the questions.

Firming Muscle

The wise for cure on exercise depend.

—John Dryden (1631–1700)

No matter what great outdoor adventure you are planning, whether it is paddling off the Alaskan shore in a sea kayak, backpacking for a week on the Pacific Crest Trail, or just pitching a tent for a summer weekend of camping at a nearby national or state park, older men and women have to be physically prepared, for the joys and challenges they face in the wilderness as well as in routine daily life.

Dr. Wade Johnson, a New York internist who specializes in working with seniors, says that whether you are 60 or 90, age is not important but a sturdy body is. If your "spring training" has been walking occasionally from your car to the shopping mall, then your first exercise should be parking as far from the mall as possible—and hand-carrying your packages back to the car.

A routine that Dr. Johnson suggested includes any one or combination of the following three key elements every week for seniors who are seeking a physically active and longer life:

1. An aerobic exercise, such as jumping rope, three times a week
2. Briskly walking a couple of miles every day
3. A half-hour swim two or three times a week

He said it is important for the mature person to accept that his or her objective is not to win a letter playing on the athletic team, but to keep the older body in good physical shape.

Keeping a Nation Fit

Although the objective of this book is the health and well being of seniors through outdoor activities, it is painfully obvious that there also is an important need for younger Americans to get off their butts. In a study of the general fitness of the nation, The Institute of Medicine, the medical division of the National Academies, said flatly that we need to exercise more—at least an hour a day, twice as much as was previously recommended.

The panel said it was especially concerned about the rapidly rising number of people who are overweight or obese. It recommended that adults and children spend at least one hour a day doing moderately intense physical activities, like brisk walking, swimming, or cycling.

Dr. Marion Nestle, chairwoman of the department of nutrition and food studies at New York University, called the exercise recommendation "impractical" since 60 percent of the population is now totally sedentary. She did not believe the recommendation of the Institute would have much impact on people's activities.

This raises an interesting point: Does Dr. Nestle imply that because people today are generally committed to a sedentary lifestyle, it is futile to encourage a more vigorous level of activity?

Obviously there is a desperate need for the nation's medical authorities to encourage an entire nation to add an extra hour a week into a life improving exercise.

Of course, putting on the back pack and heading for trails or tents, or edging into a canoe loaded with food and gear for a long junket, is an honored way of exercising at any age. In addition to regular conditioning exercises, Dr. Johnson called attention to the value of special training for activities such as:

Rock Climbing

This strengthens your legs, back, torso, forearms, and upper arms. Climbers also must have especially strong fingers and palms. For hand exercises, use squeeze-grippers or squeeze a firm ball frequently. Even better, hand-milk one cow twice a day. Remember, punching a computer for years before you retired did little to keep the hands in shape for scrambling up and down rocks while loaded with 75 feet of 11mm kernmantle rope (A loose-weave polypropylene rope developed in Germany. It is widely used by rock climbers and paddlesport activists.), an ice axe, crampons, carabiners, climbing gear, and a helmet.

Technical or advanced rock climbing, said Dr. Johnson, is a sport that is not highly recommended for older seniors.

Paddling Sports

The strength and condition of upper-body muscles used in swinging a paddle are important. To strengthen the upper body, exercise with bench presses or push-ups, or carry free weights for a least a half-hour on your daily exercise walk. Dr. Johnson said there is no age limit for participation in paddling sports, whether you choose canoeing, kayaking, or rafting.

Bicycling

Dr. Edward Craig, an orthopedic surgeon at New York City's Hospital for Special Surgery, says that some back tension pain experienced by senior cyclists can be avoided by practicing partial sit-ups and pelvic tilts every other day. He also recommended a daily stint on the bicycle.

Mountain Biking

Two of the most common injuries in bicycling, according to Dr. Atcheck at the Hospital for Special Surgery, are separated shoulders and clavicle fractures from falling over the handlebars. His recommendation for seniors who are active walkers but have done little to strengthen the upper body is to spend a half-hour or so every other day on bench presses and push-ups for two weeks before setting off on a bicycle tour.

And keep that helmet on.

Backpacking

"Respiratory fitness" is the key phrase here. The goal: Prepare your lungs by exercises that stress heavy breathing, such as short bursts of hearty swimming or jumping rope. Because backpacking gear puts heavy stress on the midsection, regular exercise of the abdominal muscles is important.

Limbering Up

Flexibility of the ankles and knees is especially necessary for the older trail hikers who may be stepping across a small stream one minute, then climbing a slope covered with scree the next.

Here is one excellent "limbering up" exercise that is especially suited to the senior who is no longer satisfied with living out life as chairborne. It cannot be undertaken while indolently watching television.

Sit on a chair. Straighten the knees to raise the feet. Now, circle each foot ten times to the right, then ten to the left. Point the toes outward and then toward the body ten times. Finally, stand on the balls of your feet, raise yourself as high as possible, hold for a moment, then drop back on your heels.

Repeat ten times.

Fear of Falling

In a study of physical activities involving seniors, *Consumer Reports on Health* (April 2001) found that "if fear of fractures causes people to limit their activities, it can seriously undermine their quality of life. Fortunately, no one has to take the risk of falls and fractures lying down." It found that use of hip pads reduced the risk of breaking a hip by more than 80 percent.

More significantly, it said the "best protection is to fend off frailty by exercising regularly. Even frail individuals can dramatically boost their physical powers through exercise—particularly strength training for legs."

Leg Strength

The following exercise was developed by researchers at the Yale University School of Medicine to promote leg strength by seniors. So, put on comfortable shoes, grab a firm hold on the kitchen sink, and start:

1. Swing your hips five times in a large clock-wise circle, as if you were whirling a hula hoop. Then swing them five times in the opposite direction.
2. Stand on the toes of both feet, hold for five seconds, then come down. Repeat ten times.
3. Stand on just your left foot for five seconds, then do the same on your right foot. Repeat ten times.
4. Take five small steps to the left, without crossing your feet, while moving your hands along the edge of the sink or counter. Then take five steps back. Repeat five times.
5. Stand on your left foot and move your right leg out to the side and then back again. Repeat ten times, alternating legs.

Hiking Staff

A hiking staff is no substitute for firm muscles. Nonetheless, it is an invaluable ally to seniors on the trail. Using one or two staffs will take considerable stress off your knees and ankles. When you use yours, pay not the slightest heed to those who would ban them because, they moan, hiking staffs occasionally create a problem on a busy trail.

Although adjustable hiking staffs are available commercially, I chopped mine from a grove of hemlock trees in a friend's back yard. It is about six inches taller then I am, and has two branches, four inches apart, each about two inches long. Grasping the lower one, my forearm is parallel to the ground, which is ideal for walking. The second is about four inches higher on the staff. I cheerfully use it to reach far up and pull down a delicious fresh apple to munch on my route. Or to stretch out and drag something interesting out of the water.

I have carved a number of notches on my staff. Each represents backpacking for a week, or about 50 miles. These backpacking trips were taken chiefly in my late 50s and 60s during the 20 years I was a scoutmaster. In my 70s and 80s, my longer trips were paddling a canoe as a Sierra Club national trip leader. They ranged from 90 to 150 miles on Canadian wilderness rivers every summer.

Occasionally I rub my constant outdoor companion with oil before standing it against a wall in the basement, next to my skis and canoe paddles, where is impatiently awaits its next trip out. To reduce the risk of the staff slipping on rocks, I fitted the bottom with a small, tough rubber cap, the type usually fitted to the bottom of furniture legs.

As fond as I am of hiking with it, I can find only one advantage that a commercial, adjustable staff has over mine. It can be compressed and stuffed inside a pack when heading off for another adventure. Mine sits beside my bed, waiting for my return from a flight. They won't let her on the overhead rack beside my on-board bag.

Food

Plan a menu that is heavier on fats and proteins than a summer menu, which includes a high percentage of fast-burning carbohydrates and runs close to 3,000 calories per day per person. 3,500 calories per person per day is preferable for the winter diner.

Make certain that every meal includes plentiful liquids, from soup to tea to coffee to flavored drinks, to make up for the tendency of even active winter travelers to consume less liquid than they should. A shortage of liquid, especially for the slender person, can result in dangerous hypothermia.

Water Safety

As if there were safety in stupidity alone.

—Henry David Thoreau (1817–1862)

The American Canoe Association (ACA) has compiled a list of universal importance to all who would enjoy the pleasure of paddling, whether in a canoe, raft, or kayak, and they are as applicable to the ten-year-old beginner as they are to her 60-year-old grandmother.

Read and heed!

It's Your PFD

Even as we accept that fact that no one, driver or passenger, should sit in a car without wearing a safety belt, so it is equally true that no one should sit in a water craft without wearing a PFD otherwise known as a personal flotation device or by its more familiar name: *lifejacket.*

Put it on. Keep it on.

Consider these statistics: In 1999, the ACA found that 75 percent of all canoesport fatalities were not wearing their PFD. 98 percent had one with them, but only 63 percent wore theirs "most of the time."

Lifejackets today come in a variety of styles. The Types I and II will float an unconscious person face up, but are too bulky for those actively engaged in paddling. The Type V is worn on special occasions, such as in water rescue. The Type III is designed to be worn at all times and come in a variety of colors, shapes, and sizes. Adult and junior models are tossed into all rental canoes.

Seniors who would rather wear their own PFD are welcome with open hands by watersports stores. Select carefully, not only for color and style but also to check size and weight limits, as well as any specifications attached to your PFD.

When buying a PFD for a child, buy only ones with a head float to keep the head erect in case of an accidental fall into the water, as well as with straps that lock between the legs to keep the child from slipping out.

Okay, so now you are getting into the swim of being a well-equipped watersport senior. Of course, you bought your own paddle when you realized how important it is to have a model that matches your own style and sport choice— whether you use a double blade for the kayak or a single blade for the canoe that hangs in your garage. You also have hanging from the wall beside your craft a throw rope. This is a 50- to 70-foot-long, 9–11mm "dry" kernmantle rope that floats.

It is stuffed loosely into a "throw bag" that is about as large as two fists. In an emergency, the small length of rope sticking out the bottom of the throw bag is held tightly in the thrower's hand and only the rope still in the bag flies through the air. When throwing the bag, always aim directly at the victim, especially if he or she is floating in moving water.

Meanwhile, as a veteran of the summer waters, you always have hanging inside the bow of your craft a 20-foot length of 9–11mm kernmantle rope known as a "painter." This is for whatever use you want to make of it: a clothesline, or a sling to catch a moose or to hold up the bow of a wooden canoe while you repaint it.

Important Hints

1. Most seniors who have had outdoor experience know some type of artificial respiration, usually the old push-on-the-chest and pull-up-the-arms technique. Far superior is CPR or Cardiopulmonary resuscitation, which involves both mouth-to-mouth resuscitation and chest pressure. You can learn it from most chapters of the American Red Cross. If you learned it once, have

you practiced it in the past year? If not, do so.

2. If you are dumped from a craft in a spill, pull yourself immediately upstream of the craft. When filled with water, the boat can exert tons of pressure if it crushes you against a rock.

3. When paddling in cool or misty weather, choose fabrics, such as Gore-Tex, that are highly resistant to water. Every sporting goods stores sells them.

4. Must you be a competent swimmer to enjoy watersports? Not really, but keep that life-jacket on—on your body, not on an empty seat.

5. Respect fishermen standing up to their hips in waders. Bouncing into them is strictly unfair.

6. In a group, don't pass lead and don't fall in back of sweep. If one stops, *e pluribus unum*.

7. River signals are universal. Practice them. A paddle held aloft, in both hands parallel to the water, is a signal to stop. A paddle or helmet swung over the head in a circular motion is a signal to stop. Three blasts on a whistle means that help is needed. Holding paddle or helmet straight up means "all clear."

8. Potentials for trouble: *Not* wearing a PFD but wrapping your beer in a PFD. Paddling in rapidly rising water or water below 50° F.

Paddling in rising winds or a storm. Go ashore and wait.

9. If you are flipped from a craft and can't reach the boat, float with your feet pointed downstream. Don't stand until you are in water where you can walk safely.

10. Keep your sandals or shoes on in the craft. Sharp rocks cut bare soles.

11. For all senior paddlers, know your physical limits. When the going gets too tough, let your grandson do the paddling.

Dehydration

Drink; for thirst is a dangerous thing.

—Jerome K. Jerome (1859–1927)

We're all aware of what we do when we're thirsty: Reach for a glass of water. But if we're sweating while hiking up a mountain or bicycling and need a sip, wouldn't a so-called sports drink that replenishes the electrolytes the body loses when exercising be better for senior travelers than a gulp of ordinary water?

On the whole, say the experts, forget most of the nonsense about whether anything should be added to the water we drink. As for seniors, go for the old-fashioned H_2O. Pure water. No juices. No Coke or Pepsi. Not even an old fashioned bottle of root beer. If you will be active for long periods, add a half a teaspoon of salt in your morning cup of water. This is a virtually discarded habit today, but the salt helps the body retain water, just as it did for millions of soldiers in taking basic training in World War II.

Most seniors don't really recognize how important keeping adequately hydrated can be. Dr. Wade Johnson warns his patients that being low on water can lead to headaches, heat exhaustion, reduced stamina, and disorientation. A low level of hydration at night can cause muscle cramps, especially in the legs. If the leg cramps cause you to awaken at night, imbibe a full glass or two of water after you go to the john.

Low fluid level means more work for the body. Sweat is distilled partially from our blood. If you go too long without drinking, the blood thickens. This requires the heart to pump harder to get the same blood flow to muscles and organs. The brain is sensitive to change in fluid levels. A drop in fluid levels is one of the sources of headaches in active older people. Kidneys need fluids to function properly. When the level falls, they dump some of their work on the liver, slowing metabolism.

The average person will lose two to three liters of water per day when engaged in normal activities. This can increase to four to six liters when enjoying a high level of activity, especially in hot weather. So, how much, and how often, should seniors drink?

There is no agreed-upon amount by the experts because fluid intake depends not only upon the weather and physical activity, but also on body size as well as age. The best approach is to drink small amounts of liquid frequently rather than gulping a quart every hour or two. Too much liquid can cause a bloated feeling, stomach distress, or stitches in your side.

Research indicates that cold liquid is absorbed faster than warm fluids. Since body temperatures rise during a workout on a hot day, the body uses some heat to raise the temperature of the liquid. What happens is that cold liquid is absorbed faster than warm liquids and this helps lower the body's core temperature.

A simple test to determine whether seniors with healthy bladders and kidneys are drinking enough water is to examine the urine. A very light urine is an excellent indication the body has sufficient fluid. A dark urine is a warning: Another gulp, please.

Because we all tend to drink less than we should, when I am leading wilderness canoe trips for the Sierra Club or the American Canoe Association, or leading a winter snowshoe weekend, every participant is required to start the day with a personal plastic bottle or ancient canteen filled with water. No juices, please. H_2O! Whenever we stop for a break, I bellow loudly:

"Take a drink. We all need one."

Most lunches and all dinners on my trips include soup, normally about 12 ounces per person. Dinners always begin with a delicious camp-recipe soup cooked over a wood fire or a portable stove, and often ends with a pleasant wine. Odd, isn't it. But there's never a slop left over.

Clean Water

There's no sweat in tossing a large jug of clean water from camp into a watercraft. But hanging it over your shoulders is a special strain on seniors involved in outdoor travel, such as bicycling or backpacking. However there are two lightweight solutions to toting the water:

1. Fill your canteen with water from lake, spring, or river. Then add a few drops of potable aqua pills picked up from any drug store (plus a flavoring, such as lemonade powder, if you wish).
2. Carry a small personal water purifier when you need to refill your canteen.

It is interesting to note that drinking water from a mountain lake or a stream is far safer than most seniors believe. Their greatest fear is that untreated water is a major cause of giardiasis and similar enteric illnesses. This is actually not so, says the *Journal on Wilderness and Environmental Medicine.* The most common source is spread by direct fecal/oral contact of foodborne transmission, not by the food you eat or the water you drink. The *Journal* says: "Hand washing is likely to be a much more useful preventive strategy than water disinfection."

And this applies equally to seniors as well as their grandchildren.

As you tell your grandchildren when they hustle back from a dash to a woodland toilet behind a tree: "Wash your hands. Now!"

You too, grandma.

CHAPTER TWO

GEARING UP

From the Foot Up

Like one that . . . spies a far-off shore where he
would tread,
Wishing his foot were equal with his eye.

—King Henry VI

When it's time for new outdoor clothing, the wisest
seniors look first at their feet.

It may come as a surprise to realize how many
different types of outdoor boots are designed today
for adults in the wilderness. What you buy should fit
your feet, no matter whether you are a newly retired 60 or a veteran wilderness camper of 90, and
no matter where you will be trekking in your new
footgear.

Within the past few years, some manufacturers
finally have begun making both skiing and hiking

boots for women based on a woman's foot shape, rather than simply marking smaller men's boots as women's. This means a more comfortable fit for women, regardless of their age and the styles that strike their fancy. There also is an increase in the number of superior lightweight outdoor boots on the shop shelves because of the growing number of seniors who are buying them.

Here is a run down of how *Backpacker Magazine* classifies boots. It should be of special interest to seniors in the market for new footgear.

Double boots—Made with a molded plastic outer shell and an insulated inner boot. For winter camping and mountaineering.

Technical scrambling boots—Special lightweight, low-cut shoes designed for rock climbing.

Mountaineering boots—Full-grain leather boots with aggressive soles embedded with grooves for slipping into crampons. They have a full-tongue to minimize leakage. They should have a lightly rockered base for hiking comfort.

Trail boots—Primarily low- or mid-cut, they are designed for carrying light to moderate loads on trails. They come in a variety of fabric and leather combinations, as well as multiple seams and flexible soles.

Off-trail boots—They offer a combination of support and flexibility with heavy-duty soles and high-traction treads. The best are full-grain leather with above-ankle support, rubber rands for abrasion resistance, and minimal seams for best waterproofing.

Rough trail boots—These are a fine boot for light backpacking. They have ankle-high uppers of leather or a fabric-leather combination. Quarter- to half-length steel shanks and semi-plastic midsoles give them the rigidity to handle rough trails.

Although boots come in a variety of styles for different terrain, they also come in a variety of materials, both synthetic and leather, and are cut in a marvelous variety of cool fashions that have nothing whatever to do with how well they are made. Don't be misled by how clever they are designed on the outside. Check seams. Check treads. And check to make certain your boots, no matter what the style, are lined with a waterproof material, such as Gore-Tex.

It pays to be swayed by two criteria: weight and cost. Expensive above-the-ankle boots can weigh as much as six pounds. How sturdy will 70-year-old legs feel at the end of the trail if they tramp around in a pair of boots that weigh half a ton as opposed to a pair weighing two pounds? Well-made casual boots usually are as serviceable on all mountains and trails for the generally more easy pace of seniors as the expensive giants are.

Consumer Ratings

In an evaluation of the quality of 17 models of outdoor boots, the three that *Consumer Reports* rated in July 2001 as the highest both for men and women were, in order:

1. REI Monarch GTX: weight 23 oz., 6.3 inches high, $100
2. EMS Dry Hiker GTX: weight 27 oz., 6.8 inches high, $100
3. Nike AGC Air Tatoosh: weight 23 oz., 6.7 inches high, $85

All you seniors eager to add a new outdoor boot to your wilderness gear, notice that all three weigh only about 1 1/2 pounds each. All three were rated slightly higher than "Very Good."

However, if you actually plan a hike far above timberline and are fully aware of what is involved in backpacking across everything from icy scree to deep snow, weight is less important than the quality and construction of a truly sturdy, heavy, high mountain boot. It's also wise to avoid the newest style of walking boots, which feature a "bubbly heel." Studies have shown that the sponge-like heel may cause ankle problems.

Buy with Care

Since foot shape and size change with the years, when seniors go boot shopping after the age of 60, make certain that the salesperson measures your foot with a Brannock, a device that measures the length, width, and arch of your foot while sitting and standing. Wear the same socks that you will wear when hiking, as well as your orthotics—if you have been professionally fitted for them. After you pick out the model that satisfies you, be certain that they have vibram lug soles and heels, which your old boots in a forgotten closet never did. Sometime in the 1970s, Italian bootmakers developed this rubber-style sole and heel, which virtually all trail hikers tramp around on today.

Try them on. Go for a long walk in the store in your new boots. Make certain when walking down a steep slope that your toes do not hit the end of the boot. Satisfied? Take them home for a one-week indoor trial, with the assurance that they can be returned if you have trouble adjusting to them, especially if they are a new size for your older feet.

Before that first hike, break them in with at least 20 miles of walking on everything: sidewalk, park trail, wherever your feet take you. If you discover loose or tight spots, manipulate the tight areas to soften them, or insert a pad to tighten the loose area.

Socks

The loss of natural padding on the soles makes it more important than ever after years of walking to wear a sturdy, thick hiking sock, which is always sold in well-equipped outdoor stores, either on the trail or walking downtown. My personal favorite is the "smart wool" sock, which is available for light to major trail hiking, but excellent, well-padded socks now are made both of wool and some synthetics. In extreme cold, some backpackers and skiers will don a thin silk or polypropylene liner under their sturdy trail or ski socks.

Use foot powder. For older feet, apply liberally two or three times a day when hiking or skiing. It not only absorbs moisture but also reduces friction by keeping your feet dry, a comfort not to be ignored when the skin both dries out and wrinkles as the years go soaring along.

On the trail, a great way to protect feet is to stop every hour and soak them in a cold stream for at least ten minutes.

Seniors with the discomfort of varicose veins would do well to wear knee-high compression socks both for street wear and under their hiking and skiing socks. They improve blood circulation and help prevent varicose veins from expanding.

Changing Gear

The outdoor trade has not ignored the impact that population aging is having on what it is designing, producing, and selling for senior wilderness wanderers—from mountain bicycles to skis, and from tents to snow shoes. Outdoor clothing is lighter, stronger, and longer lasting than has ever been available before.

Wool was once the only acceptable clothing to be worn out of doors. It was warm when the weather was cold, drew moisture away from the skin when wet, and lasted for generations. As for cotton? Bah, humbug, junk. Cloth you died in. Now, check out the superb synthetic fabrics, all with some or all cloth woven out of nylon and all available for today's active people, from squalling kids to skiing great-grandparents:

Thinsulate—A polyester blend made by 3M that consists of 35 percent polyester and 65 percent olefin. It's spun into a thin insulation for use in hats, gloves, and outerwear.

Capilene—A polyester fiber from the Patagonia company. It wicks moisture from the skin to the surface, where it evaporates. It's used in underwear, garment linings, and socks.

Thermolite—A Dacron polyester made by DuPont as lightweight insulation in gloves, footwear, and outerwear.

Entrant—An elastic coating of waterproof polyurethane that breathes through microscopic holes that allow body moisture to escape but block rain from penetrating. It's used chiefly in rain gear and to make waterproof gloves.

Polartec—A name for various fabrics made of polyester fleece by Malden Mills. Polartec is made in several weights of polyester pile, a double-sided microfiber, and Lycra stretch.

Synchilla—What Patagonia calls its Polartec filling.

Gore-Tex—The most widely known insulation laminated to other fabrics. It permits body moisture to escape through microscopic holes that also prevent water from entering.

Hollofil—A hollow fiber made of Dacron polyester for lower-priced sleeping bags and outer garments. Hollofil II is the premium brand because it resists flattening better than plain Hollofil.

Microloft—A synthetic fiber made of filaments thinner than a human hair It is used in gloves, outerwear, and sleeping bags.

Microfiber—A fine, tightly woven fiber that breathes while protecting against cold; it's also called, among other names, Super Microft and Verstech.

Polypropylene—Derived from petroleum, this is a strong, paraffin-based fiber that wicks moisture away from the body. It's widely used in underwear and garments next to the skin.

Primaloft—Micropolyester fibers interwoven into a lightweight alternative to down. It's used in sleeping bags and outerwear.

A Comfortable Night's Sleep

The silence that is in the starry sky, the sleep
that is among the lonely hills.

—William Wordsworth (1770–1850)

Our great-grandparents carried a sharp ax to chop down a good night's sleep. Here is an 1800s recipe to make an outdoor bed from scratch: First, cut two poles about a foot thick and seven feet long, and two additional poles the same thickness about four feet long. Fashion them into a quadrangle held in place by driving short pegs around them. Next, fill this with a thick pad of fine twigs, pine branch tips, or dry grasses and cover with a woolen blanket. Aha! Crawl on top and wrap yourself in a couple more woolen blankets. Now, sleep.

Of course, there were drawbacks to this mattress. The amount of chopping involved was both a sad way to treat any elderly camper and brutally destructive of even the concept of conservation camping. And the complete "mattress" was never designed for one night on the trail, but rather at least a weeklong wilderness camp that involved hunting and fishing.

So today, we turn to a much more pleasant way of handling senior nights in the deep forest. Instead of swinging an ax, swing out your credit cards and buy both a sleeping pad and a down sleeping bag.

Sleeping Pads

Although air bags have long been used to separate the sleeper from the hard, cold ground, and the outdoor active old timers may still have one with their camping gear, they are next to useless for a great night's sleep, although they can be fun in the water.

Air bags do keep the butt off the cold ground, but each time the sleeper breathes, the air inside the bag circulates and the bit of warmth next to the body is replaced by the cold air next to the ground.

Far more comfortable today are sleeping pads. There are three styles:

1. Closed-cell foam, from 1/4- to 1/2-inch thick for sturdy, young backpackers. These are fine for keeping out the cold, but they do little to keep the rocks and roots from interrupting the night's sleep.
2. Open-cell foam up to two inches thick. Comfortable on the ground, yes, but they are heavy, bulky, and awkward to carry.

3. Self-inflating, lightweight sleeping pads, such as the Therm-A-Rest, which range from one to two inches thick when opened at bedtime. They contain a foam filling that expands when the bag is unrolled. The filling keeps the air from circulating. They can be rolled as tight as closed-cell foam, which does make them easy for seniors to backpack.

Senior veterans usually have specific ideas about the type, thickness, and size of their sleeping pad. If you are new to bedtime in a tent, be fussy about sleeping pads while they are still on the store shelf.

Choose the style and size you believe you want, spread it on the floor, and lie down on it to assess the comfort you will enjoy when the camp ground is as hard as the store floor. Never mind the feet stepping over your prostrate body. If your sleeping pad will travel wilderness trails on your back, pick the smallest and lightest you are comfortable with.

Today's Sleeping Bags

It's the course of wisdom to buy the sleeping bag that suits your camping style as well as your pocket book. Are you primarily a "let's go for a weekend backpacking trek" type when the summer sun is shining, or are you planning a weeklong trek in mid-winter snows? Are you traveling by canoe or bike? Or are you tossing all your camping gear in the back of your sparkling SUV before it is parked under a great, leafy bower with your tent next to it? Seniors must also remind themselves that both their mode of travel and the weather will figure into the appropriate bag for their changing bodies.

Interested in a bag of fine down? Don't fret about the cost of down. Your great-grandchildren will enjoy it when you hand it down!

Comfort Rating

Regardless of what a sleeping bag is filled with, from synthetics to down, today's manufacturers give buyers a very good suggestion of how cold the night will be before the sleeper is uncomfortable. For today's shoppers, this "comfort rating" will be found pinned to a new bag by the producer. By way of example:

For winter camping, a bag should have a comfort rating of −10° to −20° F.

The three-season campers who are out in the cool of early spring until late fall probably would be satisfied with one that has a comfort rating of 20–30° F.

For summer-only seniors, a minimum comfort rating of 40–45° F is acceptable.

If the temperature soars, go to bed with nothing on but your granddaughter's radio.

What Down Is All About

For the warmest sleeping bag with minimum weight, look first for one filled only with down. Seniors may remember when only northern goose down was considered good enough for a fine sleeping bag. Stuff and nonsense. The single important element in down is the "fill rating." This measures how many cubic inches an ounce of down will expand to fill, regardless of color or where in the world the plucked goose lived. Very good down has a fill rating of at least 600. Top rated bags are in the 700-plus range. Prices are in the plus range, too. A sleeping bag of 600-plus down, with a temperature minimum of 0° F and weighing 1 pound, three ounces, will cost a minimum of $250.

A bag filled with a top-of-the line modern synthetic, such as Polarguard 3D polyester, with the same comfort rating, will weigh about four pounds and cost around $170. For older backpackers who do not carry their sleeping bag, if the weight is unimportant look for bags filled with Hollofil, which can keep you comfortable when the temperature at night drops to 10° F. Such a bag will sell for $70, but it weighs in at ten pounds.

It's simple wisdom for seniors returning to the wilds to study the annual guides to gear published by outdoor magazines and to find if a new synthetic has been developed that approaches that of down. Who knows when a newly developed synthetic will suddenly pop up with nearly the quality of down in comfort rating and the same price as synthetics?

In all of the inquiry about weight and filling and comfort level, if you will carry your new sleeping bag backpacking, never forget the words of the old Inuit medicine man: "An ounce of feather in your pack is a pound of feather on the trail!"

Sleeping Bag Styles

Regardless of the filling, bags today come in three basic styles: mummy, semi-mummy, and rectangular. Both the mummy and semi-mummy are for singles. The semi-mummy is slightly larger both across the shoulders and in the foot.

But recently introduced are mummy bags actually designed for a woman's physical proportions, something that no senior outdoor woman ever contemplated years ago.

Rectangular bags do have a distinct advantage over the others: Two of the same size can be zipped together, a delight for seniors who would rather continue bedding together in camp, too. Some couples buy two rectangular bags of different comfort ratings, with the higher rated bag on top on cold nights and the other on warm nights.

One factor that synthetic bag manufacturers point out proudly is that if down gets wet, the sleeping bag is about as useless as a wet towel until it finally dries, whereas a wet synthetic bag can be wrung out and retains its loft, although its comfort rating slips until it is dry.

Is the fear of wet reason enough to enjoy only a synthetic bag? Not for me. I've carried only down sleeping bags for a half-century and only once did a corner of the bag get wet. Treat your bag carefully in camp. Make certain it is not tossed onto a damp or wet tent floor, and when on the trail or in the canoe stuff it into its own plastic, waterproof sack.

Sleeping Bag Care

Even you veterans sometimes forget how to treat your sleeping bag. So, read on:

All sleeping bags absorb moisture from the weary sleeper at night. By dawn's early light, the camper should shake out his or her sleeping bag and hang it in the morning sun to dry thoroughly. If the morning air is humid, hang it out briefly when making camp in the evening, but don't forget it is hanging outside when the dew falls. Down bags should be shaken thoroughly and placed inside the tent at least an hour before bedtime so the down expands to its fullest, but this is not important for synthetic bags.

Unless your tent has a flooring that does not absorb water, the newest concept is to place a light plastic or waterproof sheet the size of the tent under the tent to keep everything inside dry, including sleeping bags, whether synthetic or down.

When stored at home, down bags must be in a loose bag or simply hung over a clothesline in a room that is always dry.

Warning: The wrong laundering can ruin any bag's fill, whether it is down or synthetic. To wash a synthetic bag, follow the manufacturer's recommendations. To clean down:

1. Do not have it dry cleaned unless the cleaner uses a solvent specifically approved for cleaning down. This is quite unusual because the cleaning fluid is highly dangerous and is rarely approved for use in cities.
2. For washing: Never use detergent. Outing stores sell a special solution specifically for washing down. If you can't find it, use only pure soap.
3. Wash and dry the bag through the spin cycle. It is not recommended to run the bag through the dryer. Handwring it if necessary, then hang the bag in an airy place, indoors or out, for a couple of days until that comfortable

guardian against the chill of a remote camp night is virginally dry. Fluff thoroughly before storing it loosely.

4. Rotating washing machines are recommended over the spiral for washing both down and synthetics because they place less pressure on the delicate seams. If you don't have one at home, try the nearest laundromat.

How often should a sleeping bag be cleaned? As seldom as possible. You be your own judge.

How Long?

Every sleeping bag eventually has to be replaced. A good synthetic bag, properly washed and cared for, and subject to moderate use—perhaps several times a month year-round—should last at least ten years. A down bag will be around 20 or more years hence.

Your eyes and your sleeping comfort are the ultimate guides into how a bag is surviving time. Are there flat spots? Does it no longer keep you as comfortably warm as it did a quarter-century ago? Well, maybe it should be replaced before you go backpacking on your 80th birthday.

Tents and Tarps

We're tenting tonight, tenting tonight, tenting on the old campground.

—Walter Kittredge (1834–1905)

For the experienced wilderness roamers, where they pitch their tents (whatever its style or age) is home. What is of more than passing importance for seniors who have not pitched a modern tent is how this housing has changed with the development of new fabrics and designs that were unthought of when today's seniors were camping as teenagers.

Two or three times each summer when I was growing up in Pocatello, Idaho, then a small western town at the foot of 6,000–7,000 foot mountains, my parents, their three kids, and an aunt and uncle would climb into two cars loaded with enough food for a week, a crucial card table, four lightweight chairs, personal and community gear, clothing, and two huge canvas tents, heavy behemoths known as miner's tents that each could sleep six.

After driving miles up narrow mountain roads through forests, we'd finally stop at a prospective campsite, always alongside a crystal stream, and unpack. It took a couple of hours of anguished pushing and pulling and shoving to get the tents upright, held aloft front and rear by heavy wooden poles the two men chopped down with a razor-sharp ax, and supported by guy ropes and wooden pegs that we kids chopped with a small hatchet.

Let me make another note of the high mountain campsite of the Gordons and Grossmans. None were hunters or fishermen. If there was a stray fishing pole in camp, it had been borrowed by a kid Gordon for this great summer expedition. As for hunting, all the game—from pheasant to leg of deer—that entered either household during the fall came from the best-equipped butcher shop.

On the inevitable card table between the two tents were decks of cards and notebooks. By the hour, the four adults played bridge. In truth, the women were much better than average. They were competitive players on the bridge circuits in Idaho and Utah. Their husbands were in camp merely to spend days holding cards and listening to the reasons why they were not and never would be competitive players.

Largely under the direction of Sanford, the eldest of the junior crowd, with sandwiches to tide us over until we got back from wherever our legs carried us, we were away from the campsite and bound for whatever peak we saw as soon as we were dressed.

Once up, the tents were protected from ground flood by trenches dug around the perimeters. If a mountain storm moved in, there was an instant melee as we all ran inside the tents to make certain that nothing was touching the canvas sides. Where anything touched them, water immediately began dripping in. The trenches always quickly filled with water, which almost instantly began seeping onto the dirt floors. But despite the problems, they were, after all, our tents and they were as fine as anything sold then, although there were a few canvas tents of other shapes for the more elegantly inclined fishermen and hunters.

The differences between those canvas clunkers we slept in and today's lightweight, double-wall, self-standing bubble tents are even greater than the differences between the first Model Ts and today's fancy SUVs.

Bubble tents are, in effect, two complete tents, one inside the other. They are supported by built-in poles, either high-tech aluminum or fiberglass. They weigh in only at ounces. The floor of the inner tent usually is nylon taffeta treated with a water repellent. The inner walls are taffeta or nylsilk and are not coated. This permits moisture to escape through the porous inner material. The outer tent, the rain fly, is water-repellent ripstop nylon or taffeta. The airspace between the inner tent and fly keeps the tents warmer in cold weather and cooler in warm weather. Fine mosquito netting covers entrances and windows, but they can be pulled aside with a sort of draw shade.

The most popular sizes are listed by their makers as either two/three person or three/four person tents. But be forewarned: the two/three person tents are comfortable for two, not three, adults, and the three/four person tents are comfortable for three, not four, adults. There are hexagonal dome tents, and round dome tents, and pyramidal and A-frame ones. Some are large enough to sleep several adults in adjacent "rooms." Some tents have an extension to protect gear stored outside the tent. And there are tents with an outer fly that can be zipped open across the top on a clear night so that the occupants can stare into the sparkle of stars.

As a rule, the weight of the fabrics as well as the style determine whether they are summer, three-season, or four-season tents. The summer tents are basically for use only during the warm months of summer, and the three-season ones offer protection from early spring to late fall. Only four-season tents are designed for camping in winter's snow and cold.

One excellent key to evaluating a tent if you are buying one is to spend a couple of days walking through a popular campsite and query the occupants about what they think of their own tent. Does it serve them the way they expected? What are its best and worst features?

It is not the most clever idea to buy from a catalog unless you cannot visit an outdoor goods store with rows of tents on display. But when you walk into a well-equipped tent store, inspect carefully. When you find a model that is appealing, crawl inside, stretch out, and wiggle around. Must you have one high enough stand up in when changing clothes? Or will you be comfortable in one with less height and less weight?

Finally, take into account when and where you will use it. Will it travel in a car, rolled up on your back, or carried in a canoe or on a bicycle? Is it for summer camping only, for spring to fall, or is it a four-season model? The cost for self-supporting bubble tents will range from around $150 for summer weather models to $500-plus for sturdy winter models.

All other factors considered, it's wilderness smart to buy the smallest, lightest tent with which you will be comfortable. The smaller the tent, the less impact it will have on a campsite and the easiest it will be to find an acceptable space to pitch it.

Tents come in earth tones as well as rainbow hues. Some purists argue that a tent's color has a visual impact on the environment, and seniors who prefer to blend with the environment should select a neutral hue. But if there are grandchildren involved, go for a bright color that is far easier for a child to find after wandering away from camp.

For older campers not used to a self-supporting tent, set up your new tent in the backyard. Familiarize yourself with how the poles are fashioned and where they go. Then take out the hose and give the tent a good soaking to check for seam leaks, which must be sealed before the rain sweeps across the plains.

Today, many campers carry a plastic sheet about the size of the tent floor to use as an extra ground cloth on which the tent is erected. Take care if you use one to make certain it is completely under the tent so that rain will not pour under the flooring and stay there.

Tent Care

Keep your tent clean, inside and out. Wise seniors will carry a tiny whiskbroom and small sponge to clean up any sand or grit that is dragged in.

In pitching a tent, clear the ground under it carefully to avoid branches or rocks that can tear the tent flooring. When you take your tent down, scatter the normal ground detritus over the tent site to avoid that "slept here" look.

Patch any rips or tears the moment they are discovered with sealing tape, which many stores provide. If none is at hand, seal them with duct tape. Most states now have laws that require that tents must be made of flame-retardant materials, but this will not protect the fabric from sparks if you pitch it close to or downwind from the camp fire. Avoid fires of any type, from charcoal to portable gas stoves, inside a tent. Not only can they set a tent ablaze accidentally, but they also may cause asphyxiation by consuming all of the oxygen in the tent.

When hanging gear in camp, do not hang it on your tent. The weight of the gear may pull seams apart. Hang everything on a nearby branch or a rope clothesline slung, not nailed, between two trees. When packing a tent before moving on, some campers will fold a tent carefully along the lines where it was first folded when purchased. However, the experts recommend that tents be rolled or stuffed to avoid damaging the original folding lines.

Once home, every tent should be opened and hung in a dry place to evaporate collected moisture. Only when it is fully dry should it be placed loosely in an oversize bag or left hanging in dry air.

Tarps

There are the hardy souls who will pitch a tarp over a rope and sleep under it. But they are not any 70- or 80-year-old seniors whom I know.

For those tempted by such insanity, a tarp as a tent may be satisfactory in a warm, breezy climate when mosquitoes and black flies are virtually nonexistent, but it is a foul thing to be buzzed and bitten awake at four o'clock in the morning.

Tarps do have a wonderful value, though, to protect an open site where you will dine. Or to pitch over a tent to keep out summer heat. Or to hang from two trees in the woods to conceal a place to shit. My favorite tarp material is Egyptian long staple cotton. It is sturdy, waterproof, and lighter, square foot for square foot, than a plastic tarp. A 9′×9′ tarp is a fine size for a small group of six or eight. A useful camp tarp will have grommets along the sides and the corners, and a molded center hole so it can be held aloft by a sliding pole, if necessary.

A final word about tent or tarp pegs: Carry a few inexpensive metal or plastic ones, which are available at every outdoor goods store. Do not chop them from fresh wood branches. Today, that's a firm *No-No*.

Maps in the Wilds

Alone, alone, all, all alone;
Alone on a wide, wide sea.

—Samuel Taylor Coleridge (1772–1834)

Whether canoeing, rafting, kayaking, or backpacking by foot or bicycle, no sensible outdoor senior would even consider a trip of more than one day on an unknown route without a compass and a topographical map of the area. *Period!*

Generally, very good maps are available in almost every country. Among the best national maps are the U.S. Geological Survey contour maps, in which one inch on the map equals 2,000 feet on the ground; and Canadian contour maps of 1:50,000, in which 1 1/4 inch on the map equals one mile on the ground.

Virtually every inch of the United States is covered by trail maps of one type or another. However, if the local map dealer or outdoor goods store doesn't carry the maps you are looking for, contact the U.S. Geological Survey Map Sales, P.O. Box 5286, Federal Center, Denver, CO 80255; call 888-ASK-USGS (275 8747); or visit their website, www.usgs.gov. For Canadian contour maps, contact the Surveys and Mapping Branch, Department of Energy, Mines and Resources, Ottawa, Canada, or call 613-995-4342.

Where to Study

For seniors with little outdoor experience, the ideal place to study the terrain you will be traveling is at a comfortable table at home, not by flashlight in a rain-splattered tent where you may find yourself when studying the terrain outdoors. To be truly prepared for the wilderness, make certain long before that special trip now that you're past 60 that you are fully conversant with the use of a compass.

On the third day of a magnificent weeklong journey in northern Quebec, we would be entering a lake several miles across, and dotted with islands, late in the morning. As we began to follow our compass course, which we had laid out several days earlier, we were slammed by a wild wind and shoved far off our planned route. I assembled our five canoes and we paddled into a quiet stretch of water where we remained for several hours.

When the wind turned into a mild breeze, it was time to orient our map and figure out how to paddle through the scattering of islands and into the spot where the lake emptied into our river. So, we were several hours later than usual when we pitched our tents on our river that evening, but we weren't lost.

Trail Travel

It doesn't take a wilderness storm to confuse those who are hiking or biking through unfamiliar country when suddenly the trail splits into two or three trails without warning. First, you stop. You knew where you were a few moments ago. Second, orient your map. Now you know which way to go.

As an experienced paddler, you familiarized yourself before the start of the trip with the terrain you will be following. You made careful note that the trip began at an elevation of 1,400 feet and ended at an elevation of 1,180 feet, so your full descent would appear to be on a mild river—except (!) in one section of a quarter-mile, where the river dropped more than 40 feet. That could mean some rather rough water, and you had better be prepared to haul all gear and equipment on a portage. Aren't you grateful you heeded your grandson's advice and rented a 16-foot Kevlar canoe, weighing in at only 45 pounds?

Backpacking involves a careful reading of your route every day. How rough is the terrain? Keep in mind the mountain philosophy that every thousand-foot change in elevation adds an hour to your hiking time. Two one-thousand peaks adds four hours to the trekking you will do that day.

Oh, a Compass

Every wilderness traveler must have two—not one, but two—good compasses. Losing or breaking your compass in strange backcountry could be a disaster.

There are two basic compasses: the needle compass and the floating dial. On the needle compass, the needle always points north. On the floating dial compass, the *N* on the dial also points only north. Your choice is a matter of personal preference.

GPS

A superb technical addition for today's traveler, whether piloting his own plane or walking across a dusty desert, is Ground Positioning System (GPS), which uses satellites to locate not only where you are, but in which direction you should be heading to reach your destination, whether you will be reaching it today or next week. Every outdoor and sporting goods store has a plentiful supply of compasses and GPSs, as well as technical books on how to use them.

Among the instruction booklets I recommend are *Be Expert with Map and Compass* by Bjorn Kjellstrom, which is available through the American Canoe Association Book Service, P.O. Box 1190, Newington, VA 22122; Map and Compass: A User's Handbook, which is available through the Appalachian Trail Conference, P.O. Box 807, Dept. SD, Harpers Ferry, WV 25425; and the popular *GPS Made Easy* by Mountaineer Books, which is widely available in bookstores.

The Art of Firemaking

When the tongues of flame are infolded
Into the crowned knot of fire
And the fire and rose are one.

—Thomas Eliot (1888–1965)

There are as many ways to build fires as there are campers to light them. Four types are basic both for campfire warmth and to prepare a delicious meal over the hot coals: the hunter's fire, trench fire, trapper's fire, and Indian fire. If, over the years, you have not built one, why not try the fire that appeals to you on your next camping trip?

Here is how each is built:

Hunter's fire—The favorite for generations of campers. In years gone by, the method was to chop down a couple of trees and make two logs each about a foot thick and six feet long. They were placed in a V shape, a few inches apart at one end, and ten to 15 at the other, with the V facing into the prevailing breeze.

The fire was built between the logs. The flames were then shoved back and forth to whatever width was necessary to support pots and pans over the fire, or the camper could chop down a few young trees and build a tripod, then hang pots for stews and soups over the flames.

Today, a hunter fire still may be built, but it must be built between two dead logs or, since dead logs are not that common, between two walls of rocks that are slightly wider at one end than the other, about 12 inches high, and only far enough apart to support a grill. The narrower end should face the breeze. If a strong wind comes up, a rock or slab of wood can be placed at the narrower opening.

When breaking camp, smoke-blackened stones can be scattered in the underbrush and the fire site covered with ground debris.

Trench fire—There are times when the most avid advocate of cooking by fire cannot find rocks or logs. The solution: Dig a sloping hole wide enough to support a grill, about two to three feet long and one foot deep, into which firewood may be fed. When breaking camp, shovel the dirt back into the trench and cover the site with ground debris.

Trapper's fire—In years far gone, the usual method was to build a hunter's fire in front of a back wall, five to six feet high, made either of stones or green logs. The fire in front of the wall was for cooking. At night, the fire was kept burning to reflect heat into a lean-to in front of the blaze. A trapper's fire usually was built only for a campsite that hunters or fishermen expected to occupy for a week or longer.

Indian fire—Quite simple. The Indians would build a small fire, then surround it with long branches in a pattern of spokes radiating from the hub of a wheel. Branches were pushed into the fire as necessary. A commentary

about the way early settlers built their fires
was supposedly made by an observant Indian:
"Indian smart. Build small fire. Sit close to
cook. Stay warm. Paleface fool. Build big fire.
No get close. No keep warm. Waste wood."

Building a fire is quite easy. Really. First, make
a small stack of tiny slivers of wood and sticks on a
pile of tinder. For tinder, an excellent material is
the thin outer bark of birch trees, and peeling
off the bark does not affect the vital cambium layer.
Pitch oozing from pine trees is a natural oil that
burns swiftly. Then, atop this, place a loose pile of
larger sticks so that air will easily get into the burning fire.

As most of us know, next comes the problem of
keeping any pile of flickering twigs alight. Crouch
down, blow your lungs out, or fan the sickly flame
with a hat or frying pan. Or—what really works—
use your mouth bellows.

The native Americans invented the mouth bellows a few millennia ago, and they used a long
hollow reed. We smart senior campers carry a three-
foot-long rubber or plastic tube 1/4 to 3/8 inches in
diameter. Pop one end into your mouth, stick the
other close to the bedraggled fire, and *poof!* The fire
flares.

Finale: Clean up when you break camp. Scatter
blackened stones. Cover the fire site with ground
debris. Stack leftover wood neatly to one side.

Firewood

The chances are slight that seniors sitting
around a campfire are going to build one from

their own select choice of wood growing nearby. You make yours out of the dead twigs and branches lying on the ground. Should you have the option of selecting (or buying) the wood of your choice, here is old-time wilderness author Horace Kephart's advice:

> Best of all firewood is hickory, green or dry. It makes a hot fire, but lasts a long time. Following hickory, in fuel value, are the chestnut oak, overcup, post and basket oaks, pecan, the horn beans (ironwood and dogwood). . . . All of the birches are good fuel, ranking in about this order: black, yellow, red, paper, and white. Sugar maple was the favorite fuel of our old-time hunters and surveyors because it ignites easily, burns with a clear, steady flame, and leaves good coal; but it is too valuable a tree nowadays to be cast into fire. . . .
>
> Most of the softwoods are good only for kindling, or for quick cooking fires.

As an aside, it would make an interesting experience in learning woodcraft for even the veterans of the wilds to take with them on their next wilderness junket a book on trees and relearn how to identify them by shape and leaf.

Charcoal

Backyard gourmets and car campers have the luxury of using charcoal for grilling foods over hot coals. Many campgrounds today provide charcoal stoves, but none offer free charcoal.

Charcoal comes in two basic forms: One widely available in almost every grocery store is charcoal briquettes. These are made from charcoal of any type of wood, which is crushed, treated, and formed into briquettes. The other, which is rarely available in the local grocery store, is natural hardwood charcoal in its normal stage. This is never artificially treated. It is found chiefly at lumberyards and at an occasional supermarket, many of which sell it in 20-pound sacks.

For our charcoal grilling, we use only the natural hickory, which adds a delicate, tantalizing flavor to whatever you toss on the grill.

Stoves

Without belaboring the obvious for veteran campers, a camp stove is an essential. How about cooking when the Forest Service bear says: "Fire hazard. No fires allowed"? Or camping in a desert area of the southwest where there are a few hundred thousand square miles of dramatic scenery, but not a single bush for a fire? The answer: camp stoves.

A camp stove makes an enjoyable, hot meal possible when hiking far above timberline; when pitching your tent on a platform to protect it, and your toes, from alligators when paddling the Everglades in Florida; when on a cross-country ski trip in midwinter; or when huddled under a shelter in a wild rain storm.

Camp stoves generally use either gasoline, kerosene, butane, or propane for fuel and are available in a variety of sizes and styles. Some are single stoves, some are paired. My recommendation for a camp stove is one that burns gasoline. Butane and propane stoves are easy to use, but they have one major drawback: They are virtually useless at temperatures below freezing.

I have long found that two single stoves are preferable to a unit with two burners, especially when the outdoor crowd numbers more than four or five hungry older campers and cooking may involve two pairs of deft hands, one pair per stove placed where each chef desires.

Llamas!

Shoe the horse, shoe the mare,
But the camel of the Andes goes bare.

On this there can be no disagreement: Neither spouse can backpack the load at 60 that he or she could, while grinning with personal pleasure at their bulging or flowing muscles, at 25. But for millions of Americans now over sixty, it does not mean an end to enjoying the wilderness, although the legs and back may need a little help during the day.

Indeed, we all are aware that as the self-loading senior wanderers grow older, they begin to abandon certain prized articles—for a smaller camera, lighter shoes, one pair of pants, one pair of socks, one small bottle of wine, and a shorter trip—long before age finally locks them into an SUV simply to move from campsite to campsite.

But then there are those unwilling to give up what they have always prized, whether in the gear they backpack, or in trekking where they wish, up great peaks, across bleak desert, or walking miles and miles through a magnificent forest. So what's their option? If the grandchildren are still too busy with their computers to go backpacking next week, most more mature backpackers have one excellent and unusual choice to avoid lightening their load below the minimum necessary for a safe and enjoyable outing:

Rent a llama!

They're great at carrying gear, and about 120,000 are available to do just that throughout every state in the nation. Where you go, llamas, once known as the camels of the Andes, can go, too! And you don't leave anything important behind, gathering dust in the basement, when the llama does the carrying.

An adult llama can carry between 75 and 100 pounds of gear or grandchildren about 16–18 miles a day. Those who rent them inevitably praise them for being easy to handle and quite approachable, and for never biting and rarely kicking, but they can occasionally spit their dislike. They tend to wander away from the camp to drop their feces, small, firm daubs that do not mar the area.

Like camels, llamas need little water and can go long stretches without a drink. They do not have hooves but have a padded, two-toed foot that is less damaging to the soil than horse or mule hooves. Llamas are welcome on all national and state parks and forests that accept horses.

It takes several hours of lessons for first-time llama renters to learn how to handle a llama for their own use on the trail. If you're intrigued by the thought of lightening your load with a llama, for information contact:

> *Backcountry Llama Magazine,* 2857 Rose Valley Loop, Kelso, WA 98626, 360-425-6495, www.kalama.com//llamapacker
>
> Greater Appalachian and Alpaca Association, P.O. Box 61, Craftsbury Common, VT 05827, 802-586-2873, www.galaonline.org
>
> White Mountain Llamas, Owl's Head Highway, Jefferson, NH 03583, 603-586-4598
>
> Maine Llama Association, 612 N. Newcastle Rd., Newcastle, ME 04553, 207-586-6800, Rmllamas@lincoln.midcoast.com
>
> International Llama Association, P.O. Box 1891, Kalispell, MT 59903, 406-257-0282, www. internationallama.org

An alternative: Rent a mountain guide service that uses llamas to carry food and gear, whether you're scrambling up the Alps, crossing Idaho's Bannock mountains, or enjoying the tremendous beauty of the great valleys from the heights of Nepal.

Mercury

Seniors who have been traveling the odd and hidden corners of the wilderness for years are the ones most likely to carry a deadly mercury thermometer that has been in their first aid kit for a few decades. If it is still around, dispose of it—but do it wisely. Don't throw it in the garbage or a recycling bin.

Most pharmacies and outdoor equipment stores that handle digital and other safe thermometers will dispose of your dangerous, mercury-filled temperature gauge safely.

The mercury in just one thermometer, reports *National Geographic,* is enough to contaminate an 11-acre lake. It is estimated that 17 tons of mercury from all sources are added to the nation's streams annually. Fish absorb the metal, and this can cause neurological damage in humans. The Environmental Protection Agency recommends limits on fish consumption because of mercury in the waters.

Replace your relic with a modern digital thermometer. It is accurate—and safe—whether placed under the tongue, under an armpit, or in the anus. They sell for $15 and up.

Foiling the Koosey-Oonek

We all know a companion who always has some totally unnecessary object in his pack when en route on the trail from somewhere to anywhere else, or in his gear when off on a fishing trip to a distant wilderness stream. And we wonder, when we spot it, what the use of that absurd article could be.

I have a friend who, in the 40 years I have known him, never paddles a canoe without carrying an "authentic" Swiss Army knife with 38 attachments I have never seen him actually use. If asked about it, he explains he carries it because one attachment may come in handy one day.

Horace Kephart, author of *The Book of Camping and Woodcraft,* which was published a century ago, noted "that amusing foible, common to all of us of lugging a useless object, from a broken mouth harp to a shaving mug.

"If you have some such thing that you know you can't sleep well without, stow it religiously in your kit."

Why? Read his explanation carefully, seniors of the wilderness:

> It is your "medicine," your amulet against the spooks and bogies of the woods. It will dispel the *Koosey-Oonek.* If you don't know what that means, ask an Eskimo. He may tell you that it means sorcery, witchcraft—and so, no doubt, it does to the children of nature, but to us children of guile it is the spell of that imp who hides our pipes, steals our last match, and brings rain on the just when they want to go fishing.

Kephart said his amulet was a "porcelain teacup, minus the handle. . . . Many's the jibe I have suffered for its dear sake. But I do love it. Hot indeed must be the sun, tangled the trail, and weary the miles before I forsake thee, O my frail, cool-lipped, but ardent teacup!"

Ah, now you, too, have discovered why you must continue to take that peculiar item with you that you have "sort of carried in your pack since you found it in the alley when you were a teenager." That is how you have foiled the ghoul who is anxious to drag your shoes outside the tent on the night it rains, tries to turn on the flashlight deep in your pack, and attempts to tip over the soup when you add a chunk of wood to the fire.

My amulet is a scratched mirror I use for shaving in camp. Printed on the back is an ancient advertisement: "Venable Lumber Co., Phone Skyline 3-3411." The telephone exchange died after World War II. No matter what your talisman is, the Koosey-Oonek will never snarl your camping adventures when you pack it along.

CHAPTER THREE

OUTDOOR ACTIVITIES

Winter Camping

It snowed and snowed, the whole world over,
And swept the world from end to end.
A candle burned on the table;
A candle burned.

—Boris Pasternak (1890–1960)

There's a quiet glory in pitching a tent when the
snows are deep and the woodlands are empty of
other humans. For the seniors who have not yet
traveled by foot, snowshoe, or cross-country ski
across the snows to set up a winter camp, the experience cannot be described. It must be enjoyed.
But to luxuriate in such a salubrious experience,
go prepared. Fully prepared. And bring your camera.

Our first winter camp was, in simple, a disaster. We had on the wrong boots for hiking in snow. We used a small canvas miner's tent and a camp stove that was not fueled for gasoline, which burns no matter what the temperature, but for butane, which is almost useless at temperatures below freezing.

Our planned three-day weekend ended as soon as we could pack up and hike back to our ancient Essex, with chains on its back wheels, at the first streak of daylight the next morning.

So, let's talk essentials—whether you are a novice of 25 or a senior of 85. We did have the first essential: We did know precisely where we were going to pitch our tent. We had camped in the same spot the summer before. Only the wilderness veteran heads across the snows without having a specific campsite in mind. We also carried an excellent compass and a contour map.

What should the novice winter camper choose for a campsite?

First, choose an area that is below the level of the surrounding ground as protection against winter winds, but not in the bottom of a valley where the coldest airs lie and where, in the event of a sudden burst of mid-winter warmth, melting snows come rolling down. If possible, choose a site in the shelter of trees, which not only deflect the winds but also are a source for a fire from fallen branches buried under the snow for those who delight in a campfire warmth as well as those who have a grill to cook over one.

Going beyond the campsite itself is the absolute necessity for a good winter tent. The finest are the self-supporting tents labeled four-season, which I described in chapter 2. They have a sturdy inner tent with a waterproof floor, an outer tent that completely covers the inner tent, and an extension fitted to the outside of the main tent for storing gear. As a rule, tents designated "two-person" actually can sleep three, uncomfortably, and those designated "four person" can sleep a crowded five.

In extreme weather, the extension flap on most four-season tents can be used as a shelter when cooking on a gasoline stove, but this stove should never, *never,* be lighted inside the main tent.

Since tent pegs are important in snow, tent ropes can be lashed to small branches or rocks buried in the snow. Tents hauled out of a backpack may collect frost, so shake the tent pieces well to get rid of any frost. Also before erecting a tent, flatten the snow by tramping back and forth on it with your cross-country skis or snowshoes.

When possible, and it usually is, dig a hole in the snow in front of a single tent for a camp and cooking fire so the heat reflected from the snowbank in back of it will be reflected into the tent. Larger groups will require a separate cooking fire downwind from the tents.

A warning: In winter, make an advance check to make certain camping is permitted. In Maine's magnificent Baxter State Park, the northern terminus of the Appalachian Trail, you must apply in advance for winter camping. A quick call to any state or national forest or park can tell you what, if any, winter restrictions apply.

Clothing

Winter boots are neither heavy leather back-packing boots nor rigid ski boots. They are a warmly designed boot lined with a waterproof fabric, such as Gore-Tex. Plastic mountaineering boots are popular. Virtually all outdoor equipment stores carry them. The best approach: Check out the boots with a knowledgeable clerk, then buy the boots that appeal to you. Do not forget the importance as seniors to make certain that all new footwear, winter as well as summer boots, are carefully measured to your slowly changing measurements while standing in a Brannock. Finally, add a pair of down booties, which are invaluable for tramping around a snowy camp.

Long winter socks, such as those worn by skiers, are a necessity. An inner sock of polypropylene or silk is a comfort in extremely cold weather. For underwear, the modern heat-retaining fabrics are a wonder to wear. If these are not available, wear only wool, never cotton. Silk also is excellent under the underwear for added warmth. Waterproof gloves are a winter gratification, but in any case gloves are a basic. So is a wool neck scarf. In cold, cold, cold weather, outer garments—pants and coat filled with 100 percent down with a rating of no less than 600—are a sincere pleasure. Otherwise, the synthetic fabrics now available for winter garments are excellent.

A few pieces of extra clothing—you make the choice—can be important.

Remember to top your knot with a water-resistant wool or synthetic cap with ear flaps. To avoid eye damage in the bright light of the winter sun, wear glasses with 100 percent UV A and B protection. The most effective sunglasses fully cover the front and sides of the eyes. Bright winter sun is a scorcher. For full protection from sunburn, carry a high-rating sunburn cream that also contains protection against UV A and B light.

Although few who backpack into the snows carry one, for the winter campers who drive in modern SUVs, an umbrella can be a source of relief when the unexpected snow showers arrive.

For nights in a tent, sleep on a self-inflating foam pad that stretches from your shoulders to your feet. If you use a down bag, one filled with down that is rated 700-plus is the finest and warmest for the weight you can buy. If weight is not critical and you want to purchase a synthetic bag, check the minimum temperature rating clipped to the side of the bag.

There are several methods of adding extra warmth on a worse than chilly night. Those who travel by dog sled measure the brutal cold by "dog." Here is how:

> Putting the lead dog inside your shelter for warmth is a "one dog night."
> A "two dog night" requires the lead plus his best friend to cozy up beside you.
> And crowding in one more is, but of course, a "three dog night."

Today we have some additional techniques for adding warmth:

> If you didn't bring a dog, wear your socks; if your feet are still cold, add your shoes—inside plastic bags.

Heat water over the dying campfire and fill your canteen before crawling into your sleeping bag with it. Ah, how delicious.

A couple of the chemical hand-warming pads that skiers use to defy the winter can be a comfort.

If you wake up at night chilled, eat some high-fat sausages as fuel to stoke up the internal fire.

Always tuck a space blanket under your sleeping pad for an added smidgen of warmth.

To maintain ventilation inside your tent, use the same system you do in the summer: a small zip at the bottom of the tent facing the prevailing wind and a small zip at the top of the other end.

In the morning, warm your boot liners inside your sleeping bag before putting them on.

Drink the water in your canteen before getting up; this will help replace the liter of moisture you exhaled while shuddering in your sleep.

Of course, the refusal of the kidneys to stop functioning at night is no reason for hikers of any age, whether 19 or 91, to climb out of a sleeping bag and crawl outside into the frigid air. Keep inside the tent a light, plastic bottle with a large lid—an empty eight-ounce bottle for instant coffee is superb—to take care of the 3 A.M. urge.

Whatever else goes into your pack, make certain you have a flashlight, extra batteries, and waterproof matches, and reread your first aid book on what to do for frostbite before you load your gear.

The Wilderness Gang

"Hail, Hail, the gang's all here."

Unless you have had major experience when the land is cloaked in ice, snow, and challenges that are not around when fair weather breezes in, I wisely, but sternly, abjure all who seek the peaceful glory of winter not to hike off solo!

In the winter, there is safety in tromping off via boots, cross-country skis, or on snowshoes, with a cluster of like-minded friends. Indeed, the rule of three applies. Always! There should be at least three sturdy people on any group trip of any kind so that if anything goes wrong and someone is hurt, one can remain with the victim while the others shuffle off for help.

My suggestion for a new group is to start off with at least four, under the guide of a person experienced in outdoor travel both summer and winter who will have the skill of being prepared to rescue the victim of any accident—including an avalanche.

There are some older outdoor adventurers who would feel more comfortable in a group organized for winter travel by such outdoor clubs as the Appalachian Mountain Club, the Sierra Club, or the Seattle Mountaineers. There is never a doubt about the leadership qualities of such a group, but the cost per person will probably be twice that of the self-contained cluster of friends on the same wilderness jaunt.

If your excursion into the snow will involve either cross-country skiing or snowshoes for the first time, a private lesson or two beforehand is advisable—and inexpensive. A diminishing number of ski areas in the United States, but almost all in Europe, offer free lift tickets for the 70-plus crowd. A day's rental and lessons on cross-country skis or snowshoes are reasonable, and the no-fee lift ticket is a special bargain if all you want to do is practice on their groomed cross-country slopes.

Underway

Whether the gang is paddling, bicycling, tromping on foot, or cross-country skiing, the method of travel on my trips never changes. There is a lead and a sweep. No one passes the lead. None ever falls in back of the sweep. If the sweep stops, we all stop. We do not move on until all are present or accounted for.

It sometimes is frightening to hear of actual problems when a group breaks up. On a winter trip in the Adirondacks, two 16-year-olds hiked across a ridge to meet the group later. There was an accident. It took hours before rangers who were helping with the search found them. One was alive, with a broken leg. The other died in the fall down an icy slope. I knew him. I cried.

On the trail to anywhere, we stay together. We know where everyone is. One ducked into the trees for an off-trail relief. The gang waited until she was accounted for.

You do the same.

Equipment

Here is what a well-equipped winter gang of snow lovers must have for their group:

1. Camp lantern that burns kerosene, with a can of extra fuel
2. Snow shovel
3. Complete first aid kit
4. Snow probe used for searching for the victim of an avalanche or a fall into deep snow
5. 100 feet of 9mm "dry" kernmantle rope
6. Wax kit for cross-country skis
7. File to sharpen ski edges
8. 50 feet of sturdy cord for the repair of snowshoes
9. Set of crampons and an ice ax—for fun as well as emergencies
10. Repair kit that includes a sewing kit, a sharp Swiss Army knife, waterproof matches, solid fuel pellets or liquid starter fuel, a small folding wood saw, and the ever useful roll of duct tape for repairing anything from a torn tent to a burned shoe
11. Emergency flashlight with extra batteries
12. Map, compass, and GPS in their own waterproof container
13. Small sled or toboggan for hauling community gear

Oh, there's more. Now come the kitchen needs:

1. Appropriate menu, selected by the group.
2. Cook, or rotating cooks, for each day.
3. Two pots with lids, the largest of which holds a minimum of a quart of liquid per person.
4. Grill for cooking over an open fire.

5. Gasoline stove, with container for extra fuel.
6. Heavy gloves.
7. Frying pan and such additional cooking gear as a large spoon, fork, spatula, and a sharp kitchen knife.
8. Roll of aluminum foil, which can be used to make a reflector oven in front of an open fire.
9. Large plastic camp bottle with a wide mouth.
10. Each person carries a dining plate, cup, bowl, and tableware.
11. Whatever else the designated cook or cooks feel is necessary.

In addition to the individual tents, haul along a 9′×9′ tarp to protect the gang when it starts to snow as the cooks start to serve the first bowl of soup.

Food

Plan a menu that is heavier on fats and proteins than a summer menu, which includes a high percentage of fast-burning carbohydrates and runs close to 3,000 calories per day per person; 3,500 calories per person per day is preferable for the winter diner.

Make certain that every meal includes plentiful liquids, from soup to tea to coffee, to flavored drinks, to make up for the tendency of even active winter travelers to consume less liquid than they should. A shortage of liquid, especially for the slender person, can result in dangerous hypothermia.

The Camera

Of course, do the usual. Take everyone's picture. And the tents. And the camp site. What a pleasure it is to bring home photographs of snow tracks of birds and animals you have spotted. Ask your grandchildren to help you identify them. Black-and-white film is especially suited for bird and beast footprints.

Now, it's winter. *Go and enjoy!*

Snowboarding

All I could see from where I stood
Was three long mountains and a wood.

—Edna St. Vincent Millay (1892–1950)

Something not in character with maturity is infecting seniors who, for a few decades, have been whipping down ski runs—on skis. Today they are increasingly testing the cool joy their children, even grandchildren, have found on snowboards.

Seniors? Snowboarding? In fact, yes!

Because of its spreading popularity among older men and women, such ski companies as Burton, Rossignol, K2, and Salomon now market snowboards and snowboard equipment specifically for the over-forty crowd. And Jon Foster, editor-in-chief of *Transworld Snowboarding,* recently told the *New York Times* that those who object to the growing number of older snowboarders have just got to get used to it. It's going to continue growing in popularity. Three years ago Mary

Reyelts of Minneapolis, who is 50 years old, formed a group of women snowboarders in a club called Snow Broads. Most of the members are in their 40s and 50s. They have only one objective: organizing snowboarding trips.

In 1998, snowboarding was accepted as an Olympic sport and made its mountain debut in the 2002 Utah games. Since then, the sport has become accepted by almost every ski resort in the world. One of the last of the major American holdouts was Aspen Skiing Company's Ajax Mountain, which finally opened its slopes to snowboarders early in the 2002 season.

From the winter of 2001 to 2002, snowboarders increased from 25 percent of ski area visitors to 28.5 percent, an increase not lost upon ski resorts, which are expanding snowboard runs, increasing the size of their board rental departments, and hiring additional instructors to teach snowboarding.

Ski experts say it normally takes about three days for athletic nonskiers to learn to board. Older seniors in good health—some active snowboarders are in their 70s and 80s—usually pick up the sport within a week. Some medical authorities say snowboard beginners are more likely to suffer injuries than first-time skiers but, over the long term, suffer fewer and less severe injuries than skiers.

What is intriguing about the increasing age and number of snowboarders is that some analysts now predict that by 2005, 60 percent of the men and women of all ages, hurtling off the lifts for fun runs down the cool slopes, will be snowboarders.

Lessons

The quickest way to understand what snowboarding is all about is to take lessons. One promptly discovers that it is not a sport for the reckless and rude, or for cutting lift lines and using foul language. But snowboarders are set apart from traditional skiers by their choice of clothing, their snowboards, and the fact that the majority still are in their teens and twenties and do use a snappy dialogue to whip around consonants and vowels.

For the skiing seniors who are curious about snowboarding, the same rules apply as to first-time skiers who want to try the sport: Rent all the gear. Then, head for the snowboarding school. Buying comes later.

Not anxious to spend the money for the weird, baggy clothing on my first try, I showed up for my first snowboarding lesson wearing my normal ski outfit. It was a perfect learn-how-to-snowboard day. Sparkling sun. Only a light winter breeze. And at a gem of a ski area, Wachusetts, in Massachusetts.

There were four of us for the class. As I came up, our instructor, a pert young woman named April, asked me if I were "regular" or "goofy"— snowboardese for which foot I placed forward.

I shrugged. "Does it make a difference?" I asked.

"Oh, yes. It's the difference between snowboarding and falling." She explained that one way to figure it out was by a sudden push from behind. The foot that you extend to keep from falling is the foot that goes in the forward binding.

Push. One abrupt push from somewhere and I threw my left foot ahead. "Regular" it turned out is the left foot forward; "goofy" is the right.

Our first lesson: putting our lead foot into our front binding. Then April had us stand so that our feet were semi-sideways with one foot in the binding and one in the snow.

"Okay, you all look like experts. Use your free foot to push yourself forward. If you push too hard, the board could shoot out from under you. Keep your free foot close to the snowboard. Push in gentle steps to gain a sense of balance."

We started to move in a wide circle. Two of us promptly fell over. It took a couple minutes for the fallen to figure out how to get back on their feet.

Next, we learned to glide by following April's instructions: "Push with your free foot. When you start to move, place it on the board and against the back binding and glide." Before this easy maneuver ended, all of us had taken at least one fall.

Next, our feet were locked into both bindings and, as we tilted downhill, we again began to slide. To slow the slide, we were told to push down on our heels so the boards would slow to a halt.

It was time to learn the "falling leaf," a maneuver in which we moved our boards in a sort of zigzag pattern. The final lesson was to convert the falling leaf into a linked turn. As she explained: "To turn to the heel side, look to the heel side, push down easily on your heel, and the board will begin to turn. After it turns, look to the toe side and your board will begin to follow your eyes. Push down easily on the toe side. Then, look to the heel side. And the toe side."

And so we learned. Easy. Gently. Look to the toe side, slide; look to the heel side, slide. We practiced the falling leaf. Pushing our board with a free foot. The class ended. We all felt that in another couple days of lessons it would be, "Snowboard, snowboard, carry me swiftly to an outfitter where I can equip myself in the loose, sloppy clothing of the true snowboarder."

The loose clothing is not a matter of style; rather, it is essential because of the amount of twisting, turning, and bending that snowboarders do and skiers don't. Since boarders frequently drag their hands in the snow, the gloves need to be reinforced and the cuffs long to keep out snow. The boarder's parka has reinforced side panels to protect the garment when the board is hand-carried. The parka also has a longer back than the skier's to protect the butt. The jeans are huge and insulated, with reinforcements on the seat and knees for protection against the snow when falling, sitting, or kneeling.

Something Special

Not only are the boards, bindings, clothing, decorations, and cool language of snowboarders different, but so also is the shape of the runs built for them in their own special park at each ski area.

The obstacles have such names as tabletops, spines, rail slides, and the almost universal half-pipes, which are rounded trenches from 400 to 800 feet long in which the skilled swoop from side to side and practice wild jumps, spins, flips, and aerial turns that awe spectators while they glory in one helluva great time.

Senior Skiers

Announced by all the trumpets of the sky,
Arrives the snow.

—Ralph Waldo Emerson (1803–1886)

Only a poet imbued with the exultation of skiing could recognize how skiers, from the wee ones to the 90-plus ski clubbers, celebrate when a new storm sweeps the mountain slopes.

"Hey, wake up. It's been snowing."

"Lemme see. Oh, honey. Isn't that wonderful?"

"Yeah, the weather report says we'll get about another six inches. It'll quit about noon."

"Oh, I hope the sun comes out. I'm getting a little old to go dashing around in a mist."

"Come on. You just turned 60. And you're still dynamite."

"You are, too, even if you have joined the 70-plus ski club."

There's not a single word of this brief conversation that did not actually occur one morning in our condominium where we were staying for a week with another couple of older friends in Sun Valley, Idaho, to ski at one of the great resorts of this globe. Our age range: two in our sixties, one 70-plus, and one 80-plus.

We had chosen Sun Valley not only because of the magnificent skiing on the great slopes that sweep down its three mountains, one of which towers at 10,000 feet, but also because its base elevation is slightly below 6,000 feet. The base height of ski areas is important, especially for the older skiers who have lived their lives at elevations below 5,000 feet (most live below 2,000 feet). The base height is where you sleep, dine, and go shopping during the hours when you are not whipping down the slopes. It's where you live. If the base elevation is above 7,000 or 8,000 feet, as the great majority of world-famous ski areas in our western mountains are, several days of altitude sickness after your check-in is the all-too-common order of the day—especially among older skiers.

Altitude sickness usually begins at around 7,000 feet. The higher the base elevation, the more likely that it will occur. Again, it is not the height of the highest run but the height of the base where you live that is critical. A base height of above 7,000 feet generally requires several days of easy skiing for the average senior until he or she is fully adapted to the altitude.

It follows this unwanted pattern: During the first two to four days after arrival, any one or several of the following occur: listlessness, headaches, indigestion, extreme shortness of breath when skiing, diarrhea, or nausea. In extreme cases there may be vomiting, loss of sense of balance, and irrational behavior. Intelligent skiers of any age should visit the ski area's health center if the problems are serious or do not disappear after two or three days. The medics may recommend that skiers immediately evacuate to a lower altitude.

In 1992 doctors doing research with astronomers on Mauna Kea, Hawaii, which has an elevation of 13,976 feet, found that a huge increase in water consumption often eased splitting headaches. They also developed a technique that quickly alleviates some altitude problems. Take a deep breath, then hold your nose and mouth tightly closed while pushing to expel air from the lungs. Repeat several times.

Adaptation

Adapting to a high-altitude vacation begins on the plane. Avoid alcohol and other diuretics, such as colas and coffee, while in flight. Drink what under ordinary circumstances would be excessive water: at least a cup an hour. For those who know in advance that they suffer from altitude sickness when skiing a high-altitude ski area, if possible stop en route, whether you are driving by car or flying, and spend a night at an area below 7,000 feet. Do not celebrate your arrival at your ski area with alcohol for at least two days. Do maintain a high intake of delicious mountain water in its pure state, not after it has been converted to beer.

Jumping on a ski lift the first hour after you check in is not for the 60-plus gang. Wait a day. Walk the streets. Gasp at the soaring mountains. Visit the ski shops. Gasp at the soaring prices. Enjoy your first breakfast without—if possible—your morning coffee. Oh, maybe decaf.

So, it's ski time. Without aggravating any tendency to suffer the normal debilitating effects of high-altitude skiing, you're off to the lifts. But for the older than 60s crowd, go easy for the first few days.

Founding Sun Valley

Deep in the depression years of the early thirties, W. Averell Harriman, president of the Union

Pacific Railroad, had spent a couple years, as he later wrote, "working to strengthen the image of the railroad as a constructive force. . . . In my travels to Europe as a banker, I had learned of the great popularity of their ski resorts. At that time the United States had only limited skiing, and I thought . . . ski resorts might become a much-needed new industry in the mountain states."

Harriman brought over a friend he had met in Europe, Count Felix Schaffgotsch, "to search for the ideal area for a similar American resort." With a couple of aides, Schaffgotsch went sightseeing through the great mountains reachable by the Union Pacific. He visited areas that later became legendary in the ski world: Aspen, Alta, Lake Tahoe, and Jackson Hole. For a variety of reasons, he turned them all down. One fatal character of each: a base elevation of 7,500 to 9,000 feet.

Among the last areas he visited was the old mining village of Ketchum, a short distance from where the classic resort hotel, Sun Valley Lodge, now stands. To Schaffgotsch, magnificent Bald Mountain towering high above Ketchum on one side, and a flank of lower mountains on the other, would convert into a ski resort to equal any in the Alps. Above all else, the base elevation of the resort would be less than 6,000 feet.

Ideal, said Schaffgotsch. We'll build it, said Harriman.

Work on building the world's first base-to-summit ski resort began in 1935. While a new gondola was slowly being erected, an engineer who had worked on banana boats walked in to see Harriman with an idea. He wanted to build a lift that would carry skiers in chairs hung from an overhead cable from the base to the summit, the way lifts carried bunches of bananas from the shore to the deck of the banana boats on hanging forks.

"Go for it," said Harriman. The result: The chair lift was invented at Sun Valley.

Sun Valley officially opened in January 1936, stuffed with celebrities from Hollywood to Broadway. For the nonskiers of the era, which included almost every celebrity in attendance, the count had brought over from Austria a clutch of ski instructors to operate the first genuine ski school in the nation.

And it all happened because the base elevation was less than 6,000 feet.

Skiing East—Skiing West

There is far less difference between skiing the fine resorts of New England and the towering giants of the west than some people believe. Two developments are largely responsible: snow making and grooming.

Long-time skiers may remember when the western areas promoted the idea that eastern resorts were skiing on man-made ice, not snow. Why, they boasted, we have so much snow in the west that sometimes we have to shovel the chair lifts free of snow so that they run. True, as those seniors who were taken in by such nonsense, often discovered: Western resorts had natural snow—except when they didn't. And snow making in New England produced finer and longer-lasting powder snow every year. So, today almost without exception, the western resorts also have massive snow making for the winters when there is little snow.

Killington, in Vermont, has perhaps the most massive snow making of any ski area in the United States. In one night, it can blanket its major runs with two feet of powder snow. Given a few chilly nights, Killington for years has been the first Eastern ski area to open each winter, all thanks to those great snow guns.

Among seniors who enjoy long, steep double black diamonds, a study of terrain features a few years ago by *Ski Magazine* found that of the ten longest, steepest runs regularly serviced by lifts, five were in New England and seven in the west.

The over-60s crowd who may prefer long, gentle slopes will find that the longer blue and green runs generally, but not always, are on the mountains that cover the largest acreage of skiable terrain. If you are unfamiliar with a resort's terrain, check its trail maps before heading off on your mid-winter vacation.

60-Plus

The nation's economy and world events will have a long-term effect on the special world of skiing. I would not contemplate what it will be over the next decade, but never forget: Give a skier snow and the skier will ski.

During the past five years, there has been a fairly steady reduction of U.S. resorts offering lower price ski tickets for skiers 60 and older. For years, many seniors could ski for free. Then, a majority of American resorts snorted: "To hell with older skiers. Let 'em pay full price." Today in Europe, however, free lift tickets for those 70 and older is almost universal.

Older skiers would recognize it is the course of wisdom to check on lift ticket prices in advance. Maybe you could take that boyfriend if the lift prices are free, or half-price. In Europe, show your passport at the base ticket office. In this country, show your driver's license, or a card identifying you as a member of an organization of senior age skiers to take advantage of any price reduction for the older crowd.

The best known in the nation is the "70-Plus Ski Club." Membership is ten bucks a year. According to Richard Lambert, the director of the organization, national membership is about 12,500 with some 4,500 in the 80-plus range, (that's me!) and some 300 over 90. Hey, skiers don't quit young.

There are several "Over the Hill Gang" clubs, mostly in the west, whose membership usually begins at age 50 or 60. These are generally most active in arranging low-cost group ski trips in North America and abroad.

Learning to Ski

Whatever your age, there are a few important elements involved in learning how to ski as an adult: Never take lessons from your husband, boyfriend, girlfriend, or wife. Nor a smarty son or granddaughter. And, this above all, not from a friend. The only thing a friend can teach a friend is how to be a friend.

Pop into a ski school for beginners, or take private lessons from a pro. Many ski resorts offer special classes for seniors, usually on a one-week learn-to-ski program.

Older learners working with an individual instructor should inquire in the instructor's training. The number-one background: certified by the Professional Ski Instructors of America!

Senior women who have never skied with a woman instructor or joined a women-only training class for a long weekend may lack the insight into improving their own skiing that they acquire from women instructors. As my wife once said after a women-only weekend: "Women really damn well do ski differently than men. And we should. We're shaped differently. We jut out differently. Our legs aren't shaped like a man's. Neither are our boobs or butts."

Ski Clothing

Unless you're into snowboarding or cross-country skiing, you need an alpine, or downhill, ski outfit. Barring an insistent stylish desire, one outfit is quite sufficient. Pants. Jacket. Made of a modern, warmth-retaining fabric that keeps out melting snow or rain but permits moisture to escape from the body. A felt vest for unusually cold days. As for underwear, my choice is polypropolene, with knee-high wool ski socks.

Wear ski goggles with 100 percent protection against the sun's damaging UV A and B rays. Some goggles can be worn over your regular glasses. Wear a neck scarf and a water-repellent hat. For the wildly plunging and the casual, use a helmet as well. Get ski gloves. Get water-repellent snow boots for walking to the car after you take off your ski boots or slopping around town.

Two other items are increasingly popular with those who fly down mountains on skis: One is a small in-your-vest-pocket camera; the other, important for all older skiers, is a top-quality cell phone, which may or may not work in the mountains.

What you wear après skiing is your personal concern.

Alpine Skis

The choices of the leading experts as to shape and style still are undergoing changes. The number-one choice today is a ski with a wide tip, narrow in the middle, and wide again at the bottom. The best size is probably 10mm to 15mm shorter than "standard" slim skis experienced seniors once wore, say some. Oh, no, cry other voices: Cut the size down to no more than 135 mm–150 mm. Shorter is better. Except, perhaps, in two feet of fresh powder?

Whether you are a beginning senior or a veteran, plan an entire day to check the various skis available at a ski resort's shop, not at a ski shop in town. Select different designs and lengths. Talk to the experts who run the shop. Test each one you choose on the same slope from the same lift. You pick. Be your own judge. Modern ski resorts have excellent shops where you can sample, rent, or buy a variety of skis and snowboards, as well as ski and snowboard boots.

An example is the Shawnee Mountain ski area in Pennsylvania's Pocono mountains. It has a broad variety of snowboard and ski boots and can outfit 4,500 customers with everything from Dynastar shaped skis with Salomon bindings to Original Sin snowboards with Switch bindings.

My first long, narrow skis were 195 mm. My first pair of carved skis were 185 mm. Now, ski school experts tell me my skis should be no longer than 155–165 mm.

Whether your skis are new or old, if you carry them on the top of your car—whether they are grandpa's or the kids'—wrap the bindings to keep ice and dust from damaging them.

Before you start down the mountain for the first time in the winter, start in the ski shop. This is especially important for older skiers whose legs have a tendency to grow weaker and who tend to ski on easier slopes as the years slip away. Have your bindings machine checked, not just a tapping hand check, to insure that they are properly set for your age, ability, and skis. Have the skis sanded and the edges sharpened. Repeat sharpening and visual inspection every couple of weeks. A small ski file in your pocket is a welcome tool to take out bumps and bangs on the edges, either on the slopes or before you trundle off to bed.

Mountain Chill

If you feel chillier in the mountains than you did a few years back, it may be shower habits. For both men and women, shower only before going to bed, and only every third or fourth night, if you are comfortable with this. Your body oil helps you stay warmer, so don't wash it away.

If you shave, do so only every second or third night before dinner so that the oils build up on your face while you sleep. Do not scour your face with soap and water in the morning. Wipe it lightly with a damp cloth.

Carry a 35-plus sunscreen lotion on every trip. Finally, for your good health, remember to add a smidgen of salt to your drinking water. Drink freely long before you head for the lofty slopes at the mountaintop café and from your own plastic bottle of water fitted with a drinking tube for sipping throughout the day.

Boots

Until a few years ago, no ski boot manufacturer ever thought of making a ski boot for a woman. They made all boots on the same last and stamped the smaller models "women's."

Then, perhaps realizing the idiocy of what they were doing, some began actually making a woman's ski boot on a woman's last. This meant that the heels were narrower, the upper cuffs wider, and the fit substantially improved. Senior women skiers with ill-fitting ski boots more than a few years old should check out the new women's styles.

Buy only those truly designed for a woman's foot, which are comfortable for you *before* you leave the ski shop. A good fit is a good fit: It is comfortable above and below the ankle. Boots do not have to be broken in before you snap them onto your newly designed bindings on your skis.

SCUBA and Snorkel

I must go down to the seas again, to the
vagrant gypsy life,
To the gull's way and the whale's way where
the wind's like a whetted knife.

—John Masefield (1878–1967)

It was early evening when our bus from a port in north Eleuthera, in the Bahama islands, pulled up to the lights shining through the palm trees at Club Med. A small group of executives welcomed us.

"Hurry, you're still in time for dinner," someone called out cheerfully to our group, which had flown in from New York City for a week at the resort. "We'll take care of your baggage."

This was my introduction to what I had expected would be a joyful relaxed week of vacationing on sand and sun for my wife and me. Instead, it became one of my most unusual vacations: I learned how to SCUBA dive.

It actually began at the sumptuous cafeteria dinner for several dozen guests seated around a scattering of long outdoor tables. We were welcome to our table by guests who poured our choice of red or white wine. Someone asked: "Are you going over tonight?"

My wife Gail and I edged into seats with a half-dozen wine glasses in front of us. "Where?" I asked.

"Over to the medical office. You gotta get examined tonight if you want to start the SCUBA course tomorrow."

And so, on our way to our cabin, we stopped for a medical check-up, including a careful examination of our ears. This is required by all SCUBA organizations that teach beginners.

I came out grinning and Gail came out laughing. "I'm really glad you passed," I said to her.

"I didn't pass," she said, nudging me. "I'm not sure I really want to SCUBA. I think I'll just stick with snorkeling for a while."

Almost 130 people showed up for our first morning class. The cost for the course and use of equipment was included in our Club Med fee. We spent the first couple hours listening to lectures on the pleasures and dangers of diving, watched TV shorts on SCUBA diving, heard about charts and gizmos that told divers how well they actually were doing, and figured, in our ignorance, that we now knew all the basics.

Day Two

The SCUBA gear was brought out for everyone to try on. On the sun-bathed edge of a swimming pool only a couple hundred yards from the rolling waves of the ocean, we were pushed, shoved, and maneuvered into the complicated gear, then each future diver went for a brief walk in the five-foot end of the pool.

As we climbed out of our gear, the instructors patted us on the back or shook our hands and congratulated how well we looked as divers, asked us to memorize some additional information on regulating air in the tanks fastened to our backs, and then, pointing to the nearby dock and waves, said, grimly: *"Tomorrow!"*

There were a few mutterings about how learning to be a SCUBA diver was too involved or too much work. "It's worse than learning how to ski," a tall redhead declared. "So damn many things you gotta know. Even a dozen hand signals, maybe more."

"But you can't yell to another diver," I observed.

He shrugged. "I'll stick to cross-country skiing."

First Down

The next morning, about half of our original crew was on hand to wiggle, wedge, and pull on diving gear and weights as we stood on a small dock.

An instructor with everything on but his mask called out for attention. "There are a couple of right ways and a dozen wrong ways to get in the water when you have gear on. Watch me. Go in the way I do, then slowly lower yourself on one of the ropes hanging down from the dock to the bottom. Don't be alarmed. It's only 12 feet deep.

"Sit on the bottom for five minutes. The instructors will be floating around among you with the time. Try to stay seated for at least five full minutes."

I found myself nervous and panting as I let go of the rope and sat on the bottom. I was breathing heavily. In a minute, at least half of those seated on the sand began to pull themselves to the surface. It took me several minutes to feel comfortable in the water, breathing through my mouthpiece, nodding to others seated on the sand, waving to those few who waved at me. Suddenly, abruptly, I felt remarkably at ease and was enjoying myself. I had fallen instantly in love with this extraordinary sport of the oceans.

After five minutes, an instructor swam slowly along, motioning with the appropriate hand signal: Surface!

I shook my head, asking with a hand signal if I could stay another few moments.

He signaled, fine, but not now. *Up. Up.*

So, up I went.

For the next three days, we donned gear, checked everything we put on, added our weight belts, climbed onto a boat, and dove into deeper and deeper water for longer and longer dives further and further from shore with fewer and fewer in our class.

Perhaps 20 of us were aboard the boat taking us out for our graduation dive. The bottom depth was between 70 and 80 feet. There we would swim about with an assigned partner, sit on the sandy depths, examine the weird formations of nearby cliffs, attempt to sight fish formations. We would practice an emergency rescue skill we had learned—to share air with our diving buddy—and enjoy the ocean depths, as though we were exploring an unknown planet, until our air indicators said it was crucial to start up. We had learned to ascend slowly, breathing regularly, halting several times on the way up, and then busting out of the water. Alive, and already anxious to take another dive.

Of the 130 or so who signed for the course, 18 to 20 of us stayed with the program long enough to earn diving credentials proclaiming that we were qualified to rent diving suits and go into the depths—as skilled novices. My first certification still sits on the top of a bookcase filled with old, musty books, where it has been for almost 30 years.

To those interested in becoming a SCUBA diver, there are certified diving schools in almost every direction one turns—from those that teach the basics in a swimming pool to those on the shores of a tropical island.

There is a minimum age to learn: 12. There is no maximum age. The head of a diving club in Cancun snorted when I asked the maximum age. "None," he said. "Every summer for the past ten years, I've been running a week program for a bunch of seniors. I guess the youngest is maybe seventy. And they're all women."

In terms of health, a doctor's approval is usually required before beginning a course. And the ability to swim? Highly recommended, but those who can simply splash around are quite welcome at most SCUBA programs.

A question frequently asked by seniors is how often must a certified diver go diving to maintain his or her skills. In my own case, I will tell a SCUBA operation if I haven't been diving for a year and ask them for a certified diver from whom I can take a refresher dive. To me, that refresher dive to a depth of at least 40 feet is worth the modest cost—which includes diving gear.

SCUBA diving can be an expensive sport, even for those who buy their own equipment. Until you are truly dedicated to it, go diving with a certified commercial SCUBA operation and rent your equipment. Only after you have a strong, personal knowledge of every item, from weights to air tanks, is it wise to haul out the credit card. Also remember that when it comes to diving equipment, as with computers, cell phones, and almost everything electronic, anything you buy today will be outdated tomorrow.

Diving is not usually associated with cold water. Except for those specifically clothed for it, is not part of the popular dive. A temperature of 70° F is not generally considered cold, except in water. At that temperature, you can become chilled in minutes. So, do what every one does who faces cold weather: Dress for it.

Wetsuits, made of neoprene, are available in a variety of sizes and shapes from shorts to full suits, and they are popular with cold-water canoeists and kayakers as well as divers. The material gets wet but the water next to the skin does not circulate and warms the body. The cooler the water you expect to dive in, the thicker the material in the suit you wear should be.

Dry suits cover the body completely from ankles to wrists so that no water touches the body. Some divers wear a silk undergarment in cold weather. Paddlers wear a dry suit over their clothing.

A dive skin does not protect the body from cold, but will protect it from stings and abrasions.

Unless you are familiar with wet suits and dry suits and dive skins, a comprehensive sporting goods store that handles diving gear is a good place to ask questions and get reasonably accurate answers as to what you should wear and under what circumstances.

Diving? Where?

One of the unanswerable questions asked by neophyte divers is where to go for an exhilarating dive. The smartest of answers is: Do you want to go diving from a resort on an island shaded by groves of palm trees, or while sailing on a live-aboard diving boat?

If you are involved with children, friends who don't dive, or those more at ease in comfortable suites with the ocean a short beach away, check the resorts of your choice—and where the nearest diving operations are. Or is it a resort solely devoted to diving?

If you want a live-aboard experience, ask questions before you make decisions. How large is the boat? Usually those 65 feet and over are larger boats, with more people aboard and larger groups of divers. They also offer more commodious quarters. How do they arrange dives? Some put small groups in the water at different times, some put everyone in at once. Usually, there are four to six divers for each certified guide. What does your boat offer?

It also may be important to ascertain the kind of dives most likely from your live-aboard. Will you inspect ancient wrecks or will you dive in thickets of kelp, a type of underwater experience known as kelp diving? How about reef dives, which are alive with tropical fish and coral reefs?

Finally, ask for the names of at least three people who have sailed on the boat you are considering, and call them for their opinion.

Snorkeling

One of the elemental pleasures of snorkeling is that it is an easy sport to learn and the equipment is, basically, a mask that keeps water out of your nose and protects the eyes from direct contact with water, a long tube known as the snorkel that fits into your mouth and through which you breath while underwater, and foot fins to propel you while you swim.

For those who've never tried snorkeling, it's worth its weight in local currency to take a beginning lesson or two from a dive master or a knowledgeable friend. Within a couple hours, you will have learned secrets that make snorkeling a perpetual pleasure. Most dive shops anywhere in the world rent snorkeling equipment; nonetheless, I recommend you buy your own, but only after your first experience to establish whether snorkeling will become your way of watery life.

Both those who snorkel and those who SCUBA may find a couple pieces of equipment important, such as a sharp knife that is useful to cut away entanglement with reeds or ropes, a waterproof flashlight for night dives, and the best waterproof camera, whether it shoots film or is digital, that you can afford.

Except for the added gear a SCUBA diver wears, there is not that much difference between the joys that each sport offers. Looking for schools of tropical fish? Want to explore a live reef? Put on your equipment and go. The snorkeler will be ready first and get there first.

And spend less money to do it.

Paddlesports

Every man paddles his own canoe.

—Settlers in Canada, quoted by Frederick
Marryat (1792–1848)

For the seniors who glory in the challenge and the splendor of the outdoors, summer is the ultimate season to splash and paddle the rivers and lakes of the world by canoe, kayak, or raft. Strap on a helmet, tighten your lifejacket, and check to make damn certain your slim whitewater kayak is in perfect condition before whipping into the thunderous Class IV rapids just ahead. Paddle tandem across a gentle lake in a classic, handmade wooden canoe. Or enjoy a unique and unforgettable weeklong canoe-camping trip through a remote Canadian forest.

Now that you've retired, if you have not yet enjoyed the self-propelled fun of wielding paddles, it's as easy to get involved as driving to the nearest livery and renting everything you'll need to go paddling, even lessons. However, beginners, regardless of age, are well advised to know the differences between the craft they can rent or buy. These are the basics types: canoes, solo and tandem; kayaks, whitewater, touring, recreational, open, and sea; and rafts.

Canoes

Easy to maneuver, canoes are generally made of strong polyester foam and shaped just as they were when laboriously handmade by American Indians from birch bark a few thousand years ago.

Canoeing, as a national sport, really developed after World War II when canoes were, for the first time, made out of leftover military aluminum sheets. These were shaped, riveted together, and turned into canoes. They could survive an accidental battering far better than the canoes made out of wood and could be mass-produced. Some of the earliest aluminum canoes are still being paddled. It is estimated by the National Sporting Goods Association that in 1998 more than 7 million Americans seven years of age and older spent at least one day paddling in a canoe. This compares with their estimate that 3 million paddled kayaks and rafts combined that year, but that number has swelled significantly in the past three years.

Three popular sizes for canoes are the solo, or single passenger, which is a canoe ten to 13 feet long; the tandem, which is 16–17 feet long—the most comfortable for two seniors and their gear on trips of up to two weeks; and the 18–20 foot length, which is for a family with children or for heavier loads carried on long wilderness junkets.

The majority of canoes today are made out of layers of various types of plastics. A 16–17 foot plastic canoe will weigh in at about 65–70 pounds. If, as a senior paddler, you will be dragging your canoe out of the water to portage around a set of rapids, choose a canoe made out of Kevlar. It will weigh about 45 pounds. Originally developed for tires on military aircraft, Kevlar also is five times stronger than steel.

Whitewater Kayaking

This is not for novices. These slim solo boats were developed by northern Native Americans for paddling in the ocean in search of food, from fish to seals—whose skin they used to make them. They devised the Eskimo roll, which proclaims that, in a whitewater kayak, the noble paddler—from teenager to senior—also can rotate her kayak upside down and emerge alive—and right side up!

Touring, Recreational, Open, and Sea Kayaks

These are great for novices and for seniors. They resemble whitewater kayaks except that they are much wider, far more stable, and come in both solo and tandem designs. Some you sit inside, as with a whitewater kayak, and others are sit-on-top models. Don't even think of trying an Eskimo roll in them.

The key difference between a canoe and kayak: A canoe is an open craft with seats, whereas a whitewater kayak always has an enclosed hull and no seats. In an open kayak, you sit or lie down. No seats. These are quite comfortable for older paddlers on a one-day trip on modest water. In a canoe you sit, kneel, hang your legs over a gunnel if you wish, or stand to paddle.

Canoes generally are paddled by a single blade, kayaks with a double blade. Canoes for whitewater paddling are fitted with large air bags, front and rear, to keep the craft afloat in turbulent water.

Rafts

These range from huge craft that can carry a dozen shrieking passengers and a guide through violent rapids of major rivers, to small self-bailing four- and six-passenger rafts for a lot of fun. These are sturdy enough on easy water for families with infants or children, as well as seniors, and the disabled who would thrill to the ability to get aboard and head downriver.

Water Classification

Every skier on the mountain, possibly with the exception of a four-year-old in ski school, knows that a green trail is a run for novices, blue is for good intermediates, and the black diamond is a mean, steep drop for experts only. Rivers also are classified for both rapids and depth of water. Seniors must know the international rating system in evaluating unknown waters:

Class A—River or lake water with no perceptible movement.

Class I—Easy, generally smooth flowing water with only minor obstructions to paddle around.

Class II—Moderately quick water, clear passages through rocks and ledges. Controlled maneuvering important. Best for intermediate paddlers.

Class III—Difficult; high and irregular waves. Visual inspection of unknown rapids required before running; maximum rapids can be run in an open canoe.

Class IV—Long, strong rapids and standing waves; can be run only in canoes filled with flotation bags or completely decked, and whitewater kayaks. Visual inspection required; advance preparation for possible rescue is important.

Class V—Extremely difficult; big drops; raging waves, snarling rocks. Visual inspection required; all possible preparation for rescue.

Class VI—Extraordinarily difficult. Paddlers, who face constant threat of death, must have the ability of Olympic contestants.

Seniors should also know water level ratings:

L, or Low—Below normal level; shallow depth will interfere with paddling.

M, or Medium—Normal river flow.

MH, or Medium High—Higher than normal; faster flow on general gradients; best flow for more difficult sections.

H, or High—Very high; all water difficult to dangerous; only for experts with covered craft; small debris on water.

HH, or High High—Very swift water, complex hydraulics, frequent debris carried by water.

F, or Flood—Water overflowing banks, low-lying areas under water, TV crews fly overhead shooting tape for evening news. Not for any boaters except those with appropriate equipment on dangerous rescue missions.

Here is how the Appalachian Mountain Club rates canoeists:

Class 1—Beginner; familiar with basic strokes

Class 2—Novice; can handle easy whitewater strokes; knows how to read water

Class 3—Intermediate; can negotiate rapids with linked sequence maneuvers in bow or stern; can paddle Class II rapids

Class 4—Expert; has established ability to run Class III rapids

Class 5—Leader; expert; can lead a group of any
degree of skill on navigable waterways

Liveries

So, it's time to get on with turning off the highway and parking your car near the livery office
where they welcome those newly released from a
long, long lifetime of working. The 2,000 or so liveries and outfitters in the United States and Canada
range from a livery with a couple dozen battered canoes stored in an ancient barn to one that rents
everything you need to get on the water for the joy
of paddling a day by yourself or a couple weeks on a
guided wilderness experience.

A fine example of one of the better liveries is
Kittatinny Canoes, one of the largest and best
equipped on the striking section of the Delaware
river, which is protected as a National Scenic
River by the National Park Service as it wanders
through largely forested Kittatinny mountains on
the borders of New York, Pennsylvania, and New
Jersey.

Kittatinny maintains two large campgrounds and
three rental-only bases on a 100-mile stretch of the
Delaware. The campgrounds have water, showers,
playgrounds, tent sites, Adirondack shelters on
river beachfronts, and stores that sell everything
from snacks to firewood to canoeing gear. Its rental
fleet has more than 1,500 solo and tandem canoes,
solo and tandem touring kayaks, and four- and six-
person rafts. On a beautiful summer weekend,
they're all on the water by mid-morning, as are an
estimated 15,000 craft from the other 30 liveries

along this section of the river. Kittatinny's canoes are chiefly the 16-foot, 9 inch "Discovery," which is made of Royalex, a tough plastic, by Old Town. It maneuvers very well when you are paddling waters that pop up rather frequently with light Class II rapids.

Ruth Jones, president of Kittatinny Canoes, says that 15 years ago, 90 percent of her rental fleet were canoes. Then, the taste of the paddle-happy began to change. Today, the rental fleet is about one-half canoes, one-fourth are touring kayaks, and one-fourth are four- and six-person rafts, the easiest for older seniors to paddle and control.

Livery rental rates generally are, as expected, similar throughout a single region. Kittatinny's are typical of the Delaware: The rates in 2001 for solo canoes and kayaks was $31 a day. Based on two persons per canoe and four persons per raft, the rate was $26 per person per day on weekdays and $29 per person per day on weekends; third, fourth, fifth, and sixth passengers in a family raft are free. Tubing also is available. On rentals, Kittatinny provides free bus service to put-ins and from take-outs.

Paddle America

Wherever you live or travel in the United States and Canada, there are liveries and rivers. If you don't know where to locate one, pick up a copy of *Paddle America* by Nick and David Shears, a superb guide to some 900 of the liveries and outfitters that offer canoeing, kayaking, rafting, and sea kayaking.

It summarizes the facilities and services for each livery or outfitter listed.

Paddle America also offers practical advice to those who use an unknown livery: Before deciding where to spend your precious vacation time, as a senior you will want to do some careful research to ensure that the destination, equipment, food, guides, and service are exactly what you are looking for. This book, with its descriptions of outfitters, can help you. Quickly find the few whose trips most appeal to you. Older paddlesports men and women should call or write five or more companies to request brochures and information.

When you have the livery on the phone, ask some basic questions. Will it provide you with a canoe or raft that is clean, in good condition, and equipped with properly sized paddles and PFDs (lifejackets)? Will you receive instruction on paddling, water conditions, hazards, and safety? Will you need to shuttle your canoe cartop? If the livery provides shuttle, how much extra, if any, will that cost? What is the policy on refunds or rainchecks due to weather or adverse water conditions? Does the outfitter have a trip to match your level of ability? On guided trips, are the guides experienced and mature? Is the outfitter licensed by the state or certified by a trade association?

Jim Thaxton, former executive director of the Professional Paddlesports Association, says: "*Paddle America* belongs on the front seat of every paddler's vehicle, right on top of the road atlas." I completely agree. *Paddle America* is published by Starfish Press, 6525 32nd St., N.W., P.O. Box 42467, Washington, D.C. 20015.

Lessons

If you are new to the paddle, especially the older generation, a great way to have fun learning everything from basic paddling to becoming a fearless expert in canoe or kayak is to enroll in one of the nation's distinctive paddling schools. Classes range from only one day to the tremendous learning experience that comes from paddling day after day with tough, skilled, and sometimes merciless certified instructors in the one-week packages, which are complete with housing and meals and are available for group trips for paddlers of every age on every river in their vicinity.

Although they had been modest paddlers before they were married, all the paddling faded away for John and Barbara when children arrived. When John eventually retired, they decided it would be a fascinating sport to take up again. They were in their mid-60s when they signed up as students for a week in the famous Nantahala Outdoor Center in Bryson City, North Carolina. After only one morning's instruction, the two could joyfully stroke safely through moderately difficult Class II rapids on the Little Tennessee River. The Nantahala is in prime whitewater country. Advanced students test their skills on Class II–IV rivers like the Ocoee, where the 1996 Olympic whitewater competition was held, or on a wild, wild set of rapids on the Nantahala—The Falls. You'll recognize them instantly as you shoulder your way through an unruly mob that can't wait on the shore for the overturned rafts and chewed-up kayaks that lost the struggle to stay upright where the river funnels into a narrow chute of boulders and ledges.

About 1 million people have taken one or more of the Nantahala's 30-plus courses for everyone from "never evers" to "been there, done that, want more." Although senior couples may take separate courses, the Nantahala recommends instruction as a team. For information, call 888-662-1662 or visit its website at www.noc.com.

Among other outstanding schools are:

Adventure Quest, Woodstock, VT, 802-484-3939
Bear Paw Outdoor Adventure Resort, White Lake, WI, 715-882-3502
Canyon Canoeing Adventures, Steamboat Springs, CO, 888-99-CANOE
Jackson Hole Kayak School, Jackson Hole, WY, 800-733-2471
Madawaska Kanu Center, Ontario, Canada, 613-756-3620
Otter Bar Kayak School, Forks of Salmon, CA, 530-462-4772
Riversport School of Paddling, Confluence, PA, 800-216-6991
Rocky Mountain Outdoor Center, Howard, CO, 800-255-5784
Snake River Kayak and Canoe School, Jackson, WY, 800-529-2502
Zoar Outdoor Paddling School, Charlemont, MA, 800-532-7483

Any will be more than delighted to send any voice on the telephone a schedule of its programs and prices.

Great sources for less technical instructions are local canoe clubs, which are widespread throughout the nation. "You wanna become a member? Hey, you're welcome to join us. Sure, and we'll teach the whole family, including your grandchildren. We not only do paddling, but also provide fine companions for a day or a week-long trip." If you don't know where to find a canoe/kayak club in your area, if one exists it probably belongs to either the U.S. Canoe Association (Middletown, OH 45044, 513-422-3739) or to the American Canoe Association (ACA). All ACA clubs in the nation are listed in the third edition of *The Complete Book of Canoeing,* which is published by the Globe Pequot Press (246 Goose Lane, P.O. Box 480, Guilford, CT 06437, 203-458-4500). I highly recommend this book to senior beginners and novices—perhaps because I wrote it.

All divisions of the ACA provide training in basic and advanced paddling. Here is what the Atlantic division of the ACA offers: Part I is an introduction for new paddlers, covering basic tandem skills and self rescue; and Part II teaches solo skills, sophisticated maneuvers, and rescue of others. Completion of both parts makes a paddler eligible for a Red Cross Fundamentals of Canoeing Certificate.

Major outdoor organizations, such as The Sierra Club (1050 Mills Tower, San Francisco, CA 94104, 415-995-1780) and the Appalachian Mountain Club (5 Joy Street, Boston, MA 03108, 617-523-0636) offer a wide range of canoe/kayak programs, from teaching paddling skills to lengthy guided wilderness and foreign tours that are increasingly popular with today's affluent senior paddlesport lovers.

Here is a sampling of the rich variety of U.S. paddling trips offered by the national Sierra Club in the summer of 2002:

Algonquin Park, Ontario, Canada, August, seven days. Paddle famous canoe routes in Ontario's oldest provincial park. Experienced canoe campers will enjoy this journey into the interior.

Family canoe/camp in the Boundary Waters Canoe Area Wilderness, Minnesota, August, four days.

Maine Wilderness Canoe, July, seven days. Canoe along gentle rivers in the company of moose, deer, and otters.

Cape May, New Jersey. Base camp, September to October, seven days. Canoe and kayak through backwater bays and lakes.

By paddle and foot: Following the Lewis and Clark Expedition in Montana, June, seven days.

Yampa River Rafting, Dinosaur National Monument, Utah, June, five days.

Family raft adventure on the wild and scenic Rogue River, Oregon, July, four days.

For information about all Sierra Club trips, both local and international, call the San Francisco office at 415-977-5522.

Here is a sampling of paddlesport trips sponsored by the Atlantic chapter of the Sierra Club, which is based in New York (summer 2002):

Upper Ramapo river: Scenic Class I–II river. Whitewater experience necessary.

Birding and boating on the lower Ramapo river: Ten miles of easy paddling.

Nissequogue river: Intertidal wet lands with numerous waterfowl. Suitable for beginners.

Upper Carman's river: Clean-up. Make this scenic Pine Barrens river more scenic by getting rid of litter as we paddle. One day.

Now, the bottom line: When it comes to watching the true canoe and kayak experts (the world-class ones, that is), visit Mirror Lake at Lake Placid in New York's Adirondacks, the headquarters of the U.S. Canoe and Kayak Team. The athletes are merely practicing as they knife through the water in their high-tech racing canoes and kayaks.

When you are considering a canoe/kayak trip in a region where you are not familiar with liveries and outfitters, select one that is a member of the widely praised Professional Paddlesports Association (PPA), whose member liveries and outfitters must meet their stringent standards. These include annual cleanups of the rivers and lakes they serve, and renting top quality canoes, kayaks, and rafts. They must provide their guests, large or small, only with proper paddles and lifejackets that meet U.S. Coast Guard standards. Member liveries are inspected annually by a PPA committee to assure they maintain the association standards. When in doubt, always go with a livery that is a member of the Professional Paddlesports Association. The PPA is located at 7432 Alban Station Boulevard, Suite A111, Springfield, VA 22150. Their telephone is 203-451-3864 and their website is at www.propaddle.com.

Essential Gear

A few items are of critical importance in a canoe, kayak, or raft that are not always included in rentals, whether you are on a month-long or even a pleasant one-day trip. As a properly equipped senior, make certain these are in your canoe:

1. Painter(cq). This is a rope of at least 20 feet long, tied to the bow of the craft. It may be used for tying your craft to the shore, or, when not otherwise engaged, perhaps as a clothesline in front of your tent. If you buy one, I recommend a 9–11 mm "dry" kernmantle rope that floats. These are available at better outdoor equipment stores. This is a very strong climbing rope that will stand up under the strain of an emergency rescue situation.
2. An empty two-quart plastic bottle with its top on and its bottom cut off, and a large sponge, both to keep your canoe clean.
3. Water purifier or potable aqua pills to purify water, or a plastic bottle filled every morning with clean water from ashore.
4. First aid kit.
5. Contour map of the area and two compasses.
6. Paddles and lifejackets, which should be included with any canoe rental.

Backpacking

Happily may I walk.
May it be beautiful before me.

May it be beautiful behind me.
May it be beautiful below me.
May it be beautiful above me.
May it be beautiful all around me.

—Navaho chant

The backpacker is a lover of the outdoors who cannot be defined by age or sex. There are those who continue to witness the beauty of the trail weaving through the forest ahead when in their 90s, and others who only discovered the joy of sleeping in a tent they pitched the day after they retired. And, yes, there are some who have yet to discover the freedom and the splendor of a backpacking trip. Pity!

For seniors new to hiking trails while carrying their own food, maps, and tent, the most logical way to begin is to go with an outdoor organization that runs easy group trips that are ideal for novice seniors. They can be found in every state. Check the names among the list of national conservation organizations in chapter 5.

For those who prefer hiking with a few friends, make certain your group has such indispensable items as:

1. Current contour map—check the date—that clearly shows the ground formation and, if possible, the location of trails in the area you will visit.
2. Top-quality, easy-to-read compass. A GPS system is excellent for keeping hikers accurately located at all times.
3. First aid kit.

4. Appropriate clothing, including rain gear. Except when backpacking in the desert in mid-summer, avoid cotton; instead, wear all wool or modern synthetics that resist rain but permit perspiration to escape. Extra items such as a down-filled vest and a warm synthetic jacket in the event of sudden cold are advisable.

5. Backpack, with either an internal or external frame, professionally fitted to the wearer by the pack expert at the outing goods store that sells them. For a trip lasting a few days to a week, a sort of mid-size 3,000-cubic-inch pack usually is quite suitable for carrying everything except a tent, which can be tied on the outside of the pack.

6. The older the foot, the lighter the boot. Avoid those that weigh in at three or four pounds if you are comfortable in a boot weighing one-and-a-half pounds. Also get a pair of light, sturdy, shoes or slippers for wearing in camp.

7. For warm weather, bring appropriate sleeping gear, including a top-quality down sleeping bag with an outdoor rating of 30° F—a fine down bag is lighter than the best synthetic—and a self-inflating ground pad.

8. Food: I recommend a minimum of 3,000 calories per person per day and 3,500 in the winter. See chapter 4 for recipes.

9. Portable gas stove, extra fuel, and cooking gear.

10. Tent: Except when winter camping, a sturdy, summer-weight, two-person, self-supporting tent is ideal.
11. Camp essentials, such as a light hatchet or folding saw, lantern, flashlight, extra batteries, 50 feet of 9 mm "dry" kernmantle rope, waterproof matches, candle lantern, and a group tarp, for four to eight campers, with all items shared among participants.
12. Camera.
13. Top-quality cell phone, however these are not always functional in mountainous country.
14. 9′×9′ overhead tarp. It does rain, you know.

The Trail

Locating trails today is relatively simple. Drop in at the nearest sporting goods store or library and check national, regional, and local trail books which include maps, trail descriptions, and, usually, the shape and color of trail markers, as well as the location of camp sites, for those new to the area.

Trail markers may be painted on trees and rocks. The most famous is the marker of the Appalachian Trail (AT), which runs 2,146 miles from Georgia's scenic Springer Mountain to the rugged summit of Mt. Katahdin in Maine. Three to four million will hike parts of it every year. Hundreds have trekked the entire trail in a continuous hike of about six months. Its marker is a white bar, two inches wide and six inches long. Markers on other trails may be round, triangular, donut-shaped, or square, and may be of a special color and size.

The universal system of placing markers is to locate each one where it can be readily seen from the last one. When a trail turns, two markers are placed, one above the other, and either to the left or right to indicate a turn in the trail. Occasionally, there will be a painted arrow pointing in the direction of the turn. Three markers in a triangle mark the end, or beginning, of a wilderness path across mountain or desert.

Over the past 30 years, I have hiked more than 1,000 miles of the AT, usually in trips of about a week as a scoutmaster with an enthusiastic troop of boys who are always itching to get started but even more anxious to reach their final goal.

On a backpacking trip, carrying personal and community gear, plus food for four days to a week, is about the maximum weight for seniors up to about age 80 in good health. A fine system for carrying all the vitamins, proteins, and carbohydrates for all to enjoy each meal is to backpack the food for the first half of the trip, then carry the food for the last half in a car and drive along a highway that either intersects, or is near, the trail. The next supply of food, appropriately bagged to protect it from weather and animals, will be hidden in a special area about 20–30 feet from the trail. Three or four days later, your group arrives, but not to go hungry. Hike to the hidden food sanctuary and bring your next week of rations to camp. Give the empty container, now filled with debris that must be hauled out with you, to the compatible adult who will drive it home for disposal. Or, arrange for the compatible driver to bring the rations for the second half of your trip to a preplanned meeting site. Greet the driver with a meal, a sip, and the debris in plastic bags.

Rails to Trails

One of the great gifts of abandoned railroads is that, either through sale, legal action, or a simple desire to be good neighbors, there now are approximately 12,000 miles for public use under the supervision of the Rails-to-Trails Conservancy. These range from dirt or gravel paths running through a couple hundred miles of remote woodlands or sagebrush flats to paved roadbeds actually in or near cities.

The beauty of the trails left after the rails and ties are removed is that they are rarely steep. This makes them a boon for older campers who want to walk, bicycle, or backpack on them. After all, steam engines hauling freight trains once ran on them. Now, you and your friends can hike them. And walk the tunnels they once ran through and cross still standing bridges. In the more remote areas, set up a comfortable camp for the night whether you're backpacking, bicycling, or kicking snow drifts aside with your snowshoes as you travel the paths of ghost trains.

For more information and maps, contact Rails-to-Trails Conservancy, 1100 Seventeenth St., N.W., Washington, D.C. 20036, or at www. railtrails.org.

Backpacking Trails

One of the splendid aspects of the nation's appreciation of the out-of-doors is the variety of hiking, backpacking, skiing, and bicycle trails that weave their way through every corner of our 50 states. These can be a special pleasure to older seniors who have thousands of miles of easy trails to backpack. Most trails that weave through our state parks and forests are maintained by local authorities often working with volunteers, but there are some cross-country trails equal to the great sweep of the Appalachian Trail, chiefly maintained by the nation's trail lovers.

Among these are:

The Pacific Crest National Scenic Trail, which follows the crests of the Cascades and the Sierra Nevadas from the Washington-Canadian border to the Californian-Mexican border. The trail runs 2,068 miles from towering mountain peaks to semi-arid desert. For maps and information, contact the Pacific Crest Trail Association, P.O. Box 1048, Seattle, WA 98111.

The Iditarod, which weaves across southern Alaska. The Iditarod is best known for the grueling, thousand-mile dog sled race held there every March; it originally connected small mining camps and trading posts. Long stretches of easy trail for seniors can be reached by car. For information, contact the Iditarod Trail Committee, P.O. Box 87-0-800, Wasilla, AK 99687, 907-376-5155.

The Continental Divide National Scenic Trail, which, when completed, will stretch for 3,200 miles and range in altitude from 4,000 to 13,000 feet. For information, contact the U.S. Forest Service, 11177 West Eighth Ave., Box 25127, Lakewood, CO 80225-0127, 303-236-9501.

For the millions of seniors who enjoy the outdoor trails that weave in and out of all 50 states, we need our own organization. Our badge, similar to that of the 70+ Ski Club, will be a green patch of about 2"×4", bordered in white and with the following words embroidered in red:
"60+ Trail Club."
All in favor, send their approval or comments to:
Herb Gordon
P.O. Box 752
New York, NY 10025
E-mail: IHG320@aol.com
Membership involves no dues, only the cost of a patch. Conventions will be any time, any season, any place two or more members gather around a campfire.

Car Camping

Climb into a car with friends, a spouse, or a grandchild or two and tour the compelling corners of America as a senior going car camping. Once you've put the pedal to the metal en route to anywhere, it's a concept of cruising that offers a boundless variety of enjoyable options.

Why not fly there? Because looking down is not as fascinating as cruising highways and byways with a slight, gnawing thought: Where do we sleep tonight? Are trains safer? (Not if you are a skilled, prepared senior—who always wears a seat belt.) So, is there an objective for retired seniors as car campers? Not one—but an endless multitude!

A sea shore? Yes, it's a thousand miles away. Fine. Start driving.

Stare with awe into the great depths of Idaho's Hell's canyon on the Snake river, deeper than the Grand Canyon! But how long will it take you to get there? Who cares?

Or undertake an emotional journey to New York City to stare in utter dismay and disbelief at what was once the World Trade Center. Check your highway maps for a list of camping areas near the Big Apple both in New Jersey and New York.

Where you will journey on your car camping adventures is not quite as important as the first requirement for seniors carbound for everywhere: Make certain the gas guzzler really is in first-class shape. Sometimes older drivers ignore the problems of the family car. When did you last check your tires, including the spare? Make certain they are inflated as recommended either by the manual or in the door jamb, not by how they look. Use a tire gauge. Check them only when they are cold. Improperly inflated tires may look fine but can increase fuel consumption by as much as 6 percent.

An improperly tuned engine is a law unto itself. It can boost fuel consumption by 10 to 20 percent. Have your favorite garage run a quick check on your engine, which is especially important in older cars, before your adventure starts. One significant sign of the need for a tune up is a marked drop in mileage performance.

Follow your manual on when to have the oil changed, and change it religiously. Check the air filter frequently: Most drivers forget that a clogged air filter can boost fuel consumption by up to 20 percent. Another way to increase fuel consumption slightly is by storing gear in a roof rack. If you need one, buy a rack that is aerodynamically efficient.

Are your headlights in proper focus and all mirrors in good shape?

Finally, make damn certain the trunk includes all the necessary repair tools: a warning flag that can be placed upright on the highway, a heavy duty flashlight for use at night, a chain that can be used to pull a sick car, a bag of sand or ashes and a small shovel if you expect to be driving on wet or snowy back roads, and a compass or a "tell-you-where-you-are-and-how-to-get-where-you-are-going" GPS.

Night Driving

A critical factor for seniors is night driving. For many, when the headlights start shining into your eyes, it is time to relax. Drive slower. Edge over to the right. Be especially aware of how well you see cars in your rearview mirror. Adjust the mirrors to keep headlights behind you from stabbing into your eyes.

Since vision usually is an increasing problem for seniors in their 70s and 80s, consider how well small mirrors attached to your regular outside mirrors can be when you are at the wheel.

There also are special rearview mirrors that reflect a wider area than the rearview mirror that came with your car. It is not at all a foolish idea to stop in a AAA office and talk to the experts about what, if any improvement, such a mirror can mean to you.

If night vision is a serious problem, discuss with your optician the possible improvement of special glasses for night driving.

Equipment

When you are fully equipped for car camping, you have everything with you to set up a comfortable camp—anywhere. Consider what should be included for car campers, but not for everyone bound for the wilds.

Regarding tents, nothing is more destructive to a pleasant cross-country camping experience with a couple of grandchildren than a single, huge tent with flaps in front of each sleeping area. First, erecting one is a labor of sweat. Second, the monster will weigh in at 25 to 40 pounds and will stay where it is dropped—close to the automobile. Third, there is a constant effort to maintain peace inside the tent: "Hey, clean up that mess." "Go to sleep. You're making too much noise." "Ssssh. Not now. The kids will hear."

The solution is elemental. A couple of two- or three-person, self-supporting, double-wall tents, with flooring, will break a group up at night. To point out only one advantage: Suppose that you spot a beautiful camp area overlooking a lake, but it's a couple miles from where the car is parked. There's a vast difference between carrying a couple of seven-pound tents as compared with a 30-pounder to the scenic campsite.

Camp equipment can be as elaborate as you want. After all, the car does all the carrying. Consider bringing with you a camp stove, single or double, and a container of extra fuel. My only warning: Stoves that burn butane or propane are popular with car campers, but they do not burn well at temperatures below freezing. Gasoline burns as hot as hell at any temperature.

Also bring a bag of pure hardwood charcoal, not briquettes, and a portable charcoal stove; a foldaway table that pops up in one minute; camp foldaway chairs, as needed; and a small ice chest for food that must be kept cool for a couple days.

In packing for a car camping journey for a group, we use the "Gordon Utility Bag System" to keep the gear from spreading all over the car and cooking area. It consists of three bags, each appropriately labeled as to contents. They are:

Kitchen utility bag—It is filled with pots, pans, dishes, and tableware.

Food utility bag—It includes all the spices, sugar, salt, coffee, flour, tea, dehydrated milk, butter, cooking oils, and vinegar; all liquids are carried in plastic bottles. In other words, it has everything that usually comes out at every meal at home.

Camp utility bag—This is the everything-else bag and includes such useful items as a small hand shovel for toilet use, duct tape, portable saw, camp lantern, camp stove, extra poncho, 9′×9′ camp tarp, a mouth bellows of 1/4-inch tubing to keep a campfire burning, 25 feet of 9 mm–11 m "dry" kernmantle rope for camp needs, and such other items as you feel important.

All large utility bags should have shoulder straps for ease in carrying from here to anywhere. For a couple of older car campers, one sturdy bag should hold all the camp and kitchen gear they will need.

Personal equipment for car campers, in addition to their clothes and tent, should include a hat with a brim, foldaway umbrella, sunglasses with 100 percent UV protection, a toiletries kit that is large enough to carry necessary medication, an extra pair of shoes for rainy weather, a sleeping bag with a comfortable foam sleeping pad, a couple of plastic gallon containers, and extra plastic garbage bags to haul away camp junk. Also bring a backpack of 3,000 or so cubic inches that is properly adjusted for your size by the sales specialist if you buy one, a small flashlight, and a plastic canteen with a spout for car use. If you expect to be drinking water from streams and lakes, I would recommend a water filter. Carry your camera and extra film in a pack you can carry with you when sightseeing.

Bring whatever else you consider necessary. But pack light.

Underway

Is your immediate goal north, south, east, or west for your first adventure? Not important. Start driving.

Our first cross-country trek by car was an accident. Four of us, parents and kids, were driving from

Maryland to camp with friends in northern Minnesota. We decided to take a side road into rural Virginia to enjoy the verdant countryside. Without an adequate map of the area, we got lost. At noon we enjoyed the food and hospitality of a small wayside inn.

"Where y'all a-headin'?" the chef and chief counter clerk asked.

"We're going on a camping trip in Minnesota."

"Quite a distance."

"Yes."

"Where y'all stoppin' tonight?"

"I don't know. We gotta find a motel."

"Well," he said, "if you're into campin', whynch'all camp tonight at the state forest. It's only up the road a piece. They gotta lotta nice places."

Ignoring our plans for a motel, we drove instead to the camping area. It was late afternoon when we pulled in. The attendant said there were a good many places to pitch tents. It was a glorious running-around evening for the girls while we pitched tents and set up our private camp, then we drove into a nearby town for dinner. As we walked back to the car, my wife suddenly said: "Let's buy some things for breakfast and cook in camp. We've got the stoves with us, and the other gear."

So we did. Our morning started with hot cereal with minced fruit for the girls; Mom and Dad devoured scrambled eggs with crisp bacon, topped with salsa and wrapped up in tacos, and fresh coffee.

Aha. Clean up. Load up. Drive off.

When we stopped for lunch, my wife called a state park we spotted on the car map to see if they had any campsites available.

"Get here by 4 o'clock," a voice said. "Good spaces then."

We hustled into a grocery store and picked up dinner and the next morning's breakfast.

We spent a couple extra and unplanned days en route to our friends, which included a visit to the ever-thundering, numbing roar of Niagara Falls. The next day threatened rain. No sweat. That was our motel night.

Our next car camping experience was an unforgettable two weeks touring the southwest— sightseeing and day hiking in such places as the Moab desert in Utah and the Grand Canyon. It began with a flight to Salt Lake City. We brought camping essentials with us including two self-supporting tents and added a few pieces of necessary gear from a sporting goods store. We rented a medium-size car and took two weeks to complete an unforgettable circular journey, car camping our way back to Salt Lake City.

Of the other junkets we took over the years, long after the kids were grown, one included a brief tour of Yellowstone Park, where we spent the nights in trashy rented one-room cabins, then on through the mountains and tenting in national parks on our way to the endless thousands of acres of lava that cover the barren and spectacular Craters of the Moon National Monument in Idaho, followed by a visit to one of the nation's largest and most spectacular ski areas, Sun Valley. Here we spent two days on rented mountain bikes pedaling along easy trails before heading off to visit Hell's canyon on the Snake river.

Car touring the Pacific Northwest included a couple days to visit the imposing Whistler–Black Comb ski resort north of Vancouver, where we could spot glaciers above the heavy timbered slopes, and extensive sightseeing in Washington and the tip of Idaho's panhandle en route to Glacier National Park, Montana.

New Orleans and the rest of Louisiana were crushed into an all-too-short one week trip.

A Different Way of Sightseeing

What adds to the intellectual vigor of car camping, whether it is in New England, the South, or the Pacific Northwest, is to learn as much as you can cram into your brains about each region. This involves frequent stops at information booths, local libraries and, always, a local newspaper.

Your physical activities can include unplanned weekends of one or two days and occasional canoe trips arranged through local liveries. Our day of canoeing the Russian river in California ended with sipping the generous samples offered by the local wineries before finding a camping area.

For seniors seeking an added dimension to life, challenge yourself with car camping.

Start next week!

Bicycling

It won't be a stylish marriage,
I can't afford a carriage
But you'll look sweet upon the seat
Of a bicycle built for two.

—Harry Dacre (d. 1922)

The exhilaration of a couple in their 80s weaving fat-tire bicycles down a soaring peak without working their butts off to get to the top is a pleasure bestowed upon the nation's pedal pushers by the nation's ski industry.

Mountain biking in snow country is not a winter sport. When the long, groomed ski trails are coated with spring grass, almost all "mountain" resorts—remember when they were "ski" resorts?—become a biker's version of heaven.

Instead of skiing over to the chair lift or gondola you rode last winter, now you bike across a field to reach one that will carry your whole crowd, with bicycles and packs, to the summit—for a modest fee. Many offer free lift tickets to senior paddlers with bikes who are 70 and older. Purchase lift tickets at a base lodge or office. The ride up is comforting and the mountain scenery spectacular.

Don't worry about getting on and off the lifts. Those that carry bikes and bikers—and their inevitable cameras—are either detachable chairs or gondolas that slow to a mere crawl at the base so that all and their gear may board; the lifts speed to the top, then slow to a crawl for an easy exit.

Get off, stare at distant peaks in the summer sunshine, put on your helmet, and take another small drink of water—with a touch of salt. And *wow!* The mountain now belongs to the bikers who may pedal, coast, or brake down the easy green runs and the wild, screaming banshees who roar down the double black diamonds. Long may they brag.

Not only are the traditional ski runs open, but many major resorts also have groomed miles of easy trails and cross-country routes for those who want the gentle terrain for their two-wheelers in the summer. They also have bicycle shops that rent and repair bikes.

Mountain biking on fat-tire bikes with multiple gears on summer's ski terrain is only one of the pleasures cyclists have known for many years. Touring wherever you choose to go, and on the bicycle designed for what you want it to do, is your choice. Follow mountain trails. Bicycle quiet forest roads. Cruise through farmland or across lonely desert.

When you go bicycle cruising as a senior, you may choose to travel via motel or elegant resort hotel and dine in restaurants, or carry a tent for camping, with permission, in a farmer's field and dine on superb meals cooked over wood fires. Remember, there is a bicycle for you: to restore, or buy, or rent.

Selecting a Bike

For those cheerful riders over 60, if you have an old bike and are satisfied with it, pedal on. But if you are looking for something to fit your concept of what you must have in a new bike, go alooking.

First, though, be aware that older bikes, especially those not regularly maintained since your kids got married and moved off, may still be an excellent choice. But they must be checked out carefully by a bicycle shop—especially one recommended by biking friends. Then double-check your skill at bicycle maintenance with the technician. Ask him or her where problems are most apt to develop on your bike and which tools you should have in the kit hanging from the bike seat.

Once everything that needs tightening is tightened, everything that needs oil and grease gets it, and any damaged parts are repaired or replaced, have a talk with the mechanic about whether you could save a nice piece of social security money by enjoying the safety of your old bike as compared with the bundle of bucks needed for a shiny new one.

One of the pleasures of bicycling as a way of exercise for the senior citizen is that bicycling doesn't require a special type of bike. But for those looking for a special bicycle, here are the types of bicycles found in today's market:

Racing bikes are lightweight with narrow, high pressure tires. Everything about them is designed to help them go fast on pavement with no baggage. Racing frames are fun on short distances.

Mountain bikes are the most popular sellers in the past few years, according to Richard Lovett, author of *The Essential Touring Cyclist* (Ragged Mountain Press, Camden, ME). When it comes to sturdiness, they are on the opposite end of the scale from the racing bike. They are at their best when you need their strength and durability for heavy touring. But they can be improved for on-pavement touring by substituting lighter wheels and higher tire pressure.

Sport bikes are descendants from the first of the 10-speeders. They look much like them but give a slightly lower ride than the racing models. They are also better on gravel.

Dedicated touring bikes are especially designed for long haul touring on paved roads. To the dedicated cyclist, a touring bike is a truck on two wheels and it feels sluggish when compared with a sport or racing bike.

Crossover bikes are just what the name implies; a blend between mountain and touring bikes. Some are referred to as hybrids. But the crossover models vary by manufacturer. Some emphasize their value as touring bikes.

Touring

One of the pleasures of bicycle touring for seniors who enjoy pedaling with others is the number of organizations, fraternal and commercial, throughout the nation that offer every type of group riding. These range from a weekend roll to a week or a month in Europe.

National and local chapters of the following conservation and outdoor organizations run a variety of trips, including some specifically for seniors. For general information, contact:

Adirondack Mountain Club, 814 Doggins Road, Lake George, NY, 518-668-4447, www.adk. org

Alpine Club of Canada, P.O. Box 1026, Banff, Alberta, TOL OCO, Canada, 403-678-3200

Appalachian Mountain Club, 5 Joy Street, Boston, MA 02108, 617-523-0603, www. outdoors.org

Federation of Western Outdoor Clubs, 4534 University NE, Seattle, WA 98105

The Green Mountain Club, P.O. Box 889, Mont-
pelier, VT 05601, 802-223-3461

The Sierra Club, 730 Polk St., San Francisco,
CA, 415-776-2211, www.sierraclub.org

Among bicycling associations that offer trips for
older seniors are:

Adventure Cycling Association (ACA), P.O. Box
8308, Missoula, MT 59807, 406-721-1776. In
addition to trips, the ACA has marked contour maps of more than 20,000 miles of
scenic backcountry and mountain roads for
bicycle roamers. They are tremendously useful for the touring seniors who are seeking
special trails.

Transportation Alternatives, 115 West 30th St.,
Suite 1207, New York, NY 10011, 212-629-
8080, www.transalt.org. Its objective is to
provide information on protected bicycling
routes that run through cities.

Cycle America, P.O. Box 29, Northfield, MN
55057. Cycle America runs up to 25 touring
trips in the United States and Canada each
year. One is a three-month sequence of tours
that can be taken in short or lengthy
stretches. Totally, their annual trips run more
than 5,000 miles.

Check out the classifieds in sport and bicycling
publications for both commercial and noncommercial trips. Some are for only several days to visit unusual sites. Others may run from two to four weeks.
Trips range from those with a sharp limit on the

number of riders to those that will take 100 or more. The trips include those in which "you pay, we provide everything" to those in which "you bring everything."

To check out trips on the internet, visit: www.localsport.com. For e-mail inquiries, write: ilherisler@localsport.com. Many state tourist agencies also have excellent information in bicycling in their states.

Warning: Under no circumstances should you plan a trip with an unknown commercial organization without giving it a thorough background check. Ask for the names of at least five former riders. Call them and check: What happens if there is an accident? Will they provide transportation to a hospital, if necessary? What about bicycle problems? Are their trips geared to a minimum number of miles each day? If so, how many? What kind of housing do they provide at night? Or do you carry tenting gear? If a trip is canceled because of a sudden change in the weather, what happens to your money?

In other words: *Know before you go!*

Camp Touring

This really is the ultimate experience, whether you travel as a group or solo.

After a day of pedaling your own chosen route, you set up your own camp, cook your own meals, and sleep the sleep of the justly tired in your own tent. What an exhilarating trip like this involves are the same problems involved by those who climb distant mountains, paddle remote rivers, or hike trails through the nation's great forests:

Go prepared!

Plan ahead. Write notes to yourself. Memory is fragile as we stride into our older years. The number-one item to have on a personal touring trip is the finest contour map available of the area in which you and your friends will be pedaling. Analyze how qualified each senior biker will be to pedal loaded bikes on the terrain that lies ahead.

Finding campsites is no more difficult than locating camp areas when your bicycles are bouncing along trails and roads in state and national parks and forests. Finding campsites on open roads usually involves getting permission from a willing farmer to set up a campsite on his land or pedal into a commercial camp area with tent sites.

Do not forget that many canoe-kayak liveries maintain campsites for their paddling customers and also welcome pedalers.

Certainly there is no problem if you decide to spend the night at a motel or hotel. Both youth hostels and elderhostels offer clean and first-class accommodations at a modest fee. For information about elderhostels, call 877-426-8056 or visit www. elderhostels.org. For youth hostels, call 202-783-4943 or visit www.hiayh.org/homenew.shtml.

Touring Essentials

One of the certainties about seniors on a self-equipped bicycle tour is that it is totally unnecessary to buy a huge backpack and stuff everything in it before you get started. If your bike does not have one, add a rear rack. However, it will ease your load carrying if you also put one on front. The most popular is the low rider, which mounts just below the top. Next, fasten two large panniers to the back rack and two small ones on the front. Now, limiting your equipment to a minimum, practice filling them with weight equally distributed on both sides. The space above the rear panniers can be used for large items, such as tents and sleeping bags. These are attached with rope or bungee cords.

Fully loaded? Satisfied with how equipment is stored? So, get aboard and do some pedaling, but be prepared to slip off quickly and rejuggle your load if your bike wobbles.

On the other hand, many touring trips, both commercial and noncommercial, are accompanied by a truck that carries all the heavy personal equipment.

Tuning Yourself

If you haven't spent the winter skiing, when spring arrives you will need to sharpen your bicycle muscles. Here is one suggested program for seniors not regularly involved in biking:

Week one: Ride every other day for a few miles.
Week two: Ride four days, between seven and ten miles each day.
Week three: Five days of riding, 15 miles each time.
Weeks four and after: Ride daily for whatever distance you wish, keeping in mind that it's quite common for touring trips to travel 70 miles a day when on the road.

Traffic

If, indeed, it has been years since you soared off on a bike, never forget that you are not driving a car. Cars are your deadly enemy. Drivers do not always see a bicycle. Always wear a light-colored jacket or sweater with reflector tape on the front and back—regardless of the time of day. It's also intelligent to fly a small yellow flag of reflector tape from a pole attached to the back rack.

Follow the "bicycle" rules of the road. Drive on the extreme right-hand side with the traffic. Make the same appropriate hand signals you did when driving a car before the era of the flashing car lights. Your left hand is held high when turning right, pointed straight out when turning left, and pointed down when stopping.

Don't whip through red lights or stop signs. If you are not hit by a car, you can be given a traffic ticket. Also, be especially alert to parked cars suddenly opening a door in front of you.

Wind

With the wind at your back you can pedal cheerfully for miles, but when the wind shifts it becomes an adversary.

The normal wind pattern in the United States is west to east. Morning breezes generally pick up around noon. The strongest breezes are in midafternoon. When pedaling into the wind, the largest biker takes the lead. The smaller biker rides close behind or slightly to one side where the wind is least painful. When the wind is blowing wildly, you will quickly recognize why I recommend snug-fitting

clothing. Only the young do not seem at all concerned with flapping clothes.

Bridges and Tunnels

Bridges can be a problem because of both traffic
and weather. There are no barriers against a strong
wind. If possible, plan to bike across bridges in early
mornings or late evenings when the winds tend to
be lightest.

Certainly the winds are no problem in tunnels,
but the goddamned 18-wheelers are as they go
hurtling past. On busy highways, avoid tunnels if at
all possible, or walk your bikes through.

Bike Saddles

Yes, they are different for men and women. The
so-called unisex is not the saddle for older riders,
neither man nor woman. A good woman's saddle
will be both slightly wider and a different shape
than a man's. A man's will have a slight depression
in the center to avoid irritating a man's testes. All
saddles also can be equipped with comfortable
padded seat covers.

Personal Equipment

For the camping cyclist, here is a suggestion list
of clothing:

1. Cycling shoes.
2. Light walking shoes for camp wear.
3. Two pair of shorts.

4. Sunscreen lotion that repels UV A and B light from exposed skin.
5. One pair of long pants.
6. Two light-colored shirts or jackets.
7. One felt jacket with full sleeves, for when the weather turns chilly.
8. Gloves, to wear when needed.
9. A rain suit, not a poncho. You can choose from a plastic suit to fine-quality rain gear, such as Gore-Tex, which sheds rain but allows body moisture to escape.
10. Thick hiking socks, such as "mart wool," for pedaling comfort.
11. Polypropylene underwear, which is highly welcome on a cold night in a tent.
12. Two pair of undershorts.
13. Ankle clips to keep pants legs from flapping.
14. Light wool cap.
15. Helmet, a must even for 80-year-olds on a bike.
16. Light reflecting straps to fasten on your back for foggy days and when night pedaling; you may also wear the new clothing made of light-reflecting material.

General Items

1. Extra tire or inner tube
2. Patch kit
3. Bicycle oil in can
4. Air pump
5. Personal flashlight
6. Flashing light that can be fastened to a helmet or the back of a bike for night riding

7. Lock and chain
8. Sharp pocketknife
9. Two-quart water bottle, preferably a strap-on style with a tube for drinking while riding
10. Small backpack, which can be worn low on the back (optional)
11. Bungee cord
12. Toe clips or clip-in pedals
13. Rearview mirror
14. One 20-foot 9 mm kernmantle rope, for general use in a camp of several bikers
15. Carabiner, for emergencies
16. Handlebar pack for carrying maps and compass
17. Reflecting pads attached to each pedal

Creating Photography

If I could do it, I'd do no writing at all here. It
would be photographs; the rest would
be fragments.

—James Agee (1909–1955)

Capturing impressions, moods, and moments in photographs is not an accident but a skill that can be learned by the photographer of any age.

Indeed, one of the delicious delights of handling a fine photograph of your own may come as a surprise to those whose albums are routinely filled with groups and faces of friends and family in standard settings. Whether you use a point-and-shoot camera or a chic and expensive digital is not important. It's not what your hand holds, but what your eye beholds.

Before talking photography basics, however, let's look at photography as a wonderful way to put a senior's body and mind to work. Go climb a mountain. A long, long hike to the summit. Shoot from up there. Get out of the car and walk a mile or two to see if you can get a better view of what attracts your eye.

Ah, can you conceive of a more enjoyable way to be physically active than carrying a camera across field and stream to places you never thought of photographing before? Or to put the camera to a creative use with your own lighting for an unusual shot of a person or a quiet moment?

Whether you are 58 or 85, the camera is an instrument for both the physically and mentally active. But not if it only sits in your closet. Put it to creative work.

Some Basics

For the camera that uses film, it makes little difference whether you shoot black-and-white or color prints or slides. Where you buy your film and have it processed, however, can be of importance.

The quickie stop is a drug store. There is no way of knowing how fresh or old the film is, and it's quite useless to ask a salesclerk for professional advice about the film. Instead, make it a point, whenever possible, to buy your film from a camera shop. For example, color slide film should be stored only in a refrigerator, not on an open shelf. A camera shop salesperson will have a good knowledge about different films and be able to answer your questions.

Next, where do you take your film, any film, for developing and printing? Again, my recommendation is always a camera shop or lab, not a drug store envelope nor a "prints made in one hour" shop.

Your Camera

If you do not own a camera, my recommendation is to buy the best camera you can afford within your price range that has settings that can switch from manual to automatic focus. The automatic focus setting, in effect, tells the photographer, "This is the setting I will give you," which is fine under most circumstances. But there are times and moments when the automatic doesn't have the proper setting.

Consider, for example, that you want to take a photograph of a brilliant sunset. The automatic focus setting will blank out everything but the brilliant sun. However, with a manual setting, you can point your camera to one side of the sun and set the camera for the beautiful background you want to capture. Now, point the camera at the sunset and shoot. The brilliance of the sun will not blank out the background you have chosen.

A Great Shot

As an amateur who had been quite satisfied with his camera skills for many years, I finally took a special course in a form of photography I had always admired, travel photography, at the International Center of Photography in New York City. The 16 "students" in a class taught by a professional travel photographer ranged in age from their mid-30s to a woman in her early 80s. We each brought six slides to be shown, and discussed, at our first meeting.

The first slides were of a mountain lake surrounded by snow-capped peaks.

"Ah," our instructor said, after looking at the slides for a moment, "now let me tell you how you shot this. You were driving down the highway in the middle of the day and rounded a bend and saw this lake and trees.

"And you knew it would be a great picture. So, you stopped, hopped out of your car, and took a couple of shots."

The student, a man in his late 40s, smiled in agreement.

"Well," said the instructor, "that's why the light is flat. Middle of the day. Bright sunshine. Why didn't you drive back and shoot it in the late afternoon when the light is full of passion? Why didn't you shoot it from different angles? You could have a magnificent picture. But what you got," he paused, "is only a postcard."

He roamed through the class, putting up different slides, mixing praise and comments.

The first class focused on two specific items: the light by which each shot was made, and how the same scene could have been reshot for a more interesting view.

Since that first class, I am always aware of the light before I take my first shot of a scene I want to capture on film, taking into account the need to try different angles. If I feel it is something I want to capture, I shoot somewhere between the first streaks of dawn until mid-morning, then, unless it is a cloudy day, put my camera aside until late in the afternoon when the colors are at their most poignant, whether it is summer or mid-winter.

I walk around, shoot several here and there. For a special scene, I follow the rule of three: I take one shot precisely where my meter tells me to set the camera, then a second shot one f-stop faster, and a third shot an f-stop slower.

I shoot a wide angle to encompass the scene, always with something in the foreground to emphasize the depth and beauty of the scene. A rock. A branch. A fence. A wave. Then I try shooting both horizontally and vertically. And, when possible, from an elevation. But, above all, I keep the camera level unless I tilt for effect.

One not insignificant factor about age and photography: shaking hand. To avoid this affecting your pictures, the best solution is a tripod. A secondary choice is a monopod with height adjustment. Without either one, brace your camera against something solid—such as a wall or tree. When I have nothing to keep my hand steady, I set my shutter speed at 125, whether I am shooting a bouncing puppy, a scenic mountain, or the shadow of a towering building.

When roaming the back lands, whether by foot, car, llama, kayak, or raft, I urge every photographer to keep the camera loaded. And handy. When that striking scene captures your eye, shoot. Then shoot more. Be a spendthrift with your film. Shoot it several times. Don't hoard film.

I learned significant aspects of photography from that course in photography. There are fine photographic schools, both independent as well as many that are associated with colleges and universities throughout the nation. They offer a variety of courses in all areas of photography. If you haven't taken a course in a branch of photography that interests you, get up and go register! You're not too old for that, are you?

Capturing People

It's annoying to capture those you love on film and then have to guess whom that person is. So, shoot close enough to capture her full identity before you snap. Don't lop off the chin or cut off the head just above the eyes. A full-length body shot does not end at the knees. Pick the entire picture you want before you snap the camera.

When photographing people, whether at a dinner or in camp, remember that each setting deserves at least three shots from slightly different angles. Focus so that the people fill the camera. Use your film. Don't hoard it in the camera or your pocket.

Action

When I want to capture the clouds from my plane in flight, I shoot only color slides on professional film. Again and again. So, maybe I shoot a dozen. I have no regrets. The one or two engrossing photos I captured will be displayed on professional prints hanging in my home.

To capture high-speed action, such as a skier zooming down a steep pitch or a raft bouncing through foaming waves, plan in advance. Estimate the speed and f stop you will use, and where you will be focusing when the action flashes into view. If you have an auto-focus camera with a motor drive or a digital, fine. Also, using a flash generally offers red-eye reduction. But even without an elegant system, be ready for that instant moment when it's time to snap. And have your outstanding photos enlarged.

When the weather is cold, it's not necessary to keep your camera inside your jacket, but don't breathe on a chilly lens. Keep an extra set of batteries in your parka. Battery life has improved with the use of smaller lithium cells rather than alkaline. Although more expensive, lithium batteries are the longest lasting in summer or winter.

Film Rating

The higher the rating, the faster the film. The lower the rating the finer the grain of the film. For those major enlargements, when the light is kind, I shoot with an ASA of 50, which is usually available as slide film. Generally, the newest professional slide film with an ASA of 100 is almost as fine grain as the ASA 50. Under a professional lab, these will produce 16"×24" or larger prints with a brilliant clarity. The higher speed films, such as ASA 200, 400, 800, and 1600, which may be essential in a dim light or in action photography, are coarser-grained and are not quite as kind to a large blow-up.

APS

The newest member of the point-and-shoot film cameras is the Advanced Photo System, or APS. For

$100 and up, you can get one with a zoom lens and one with a choice between a camera that accepts 35mm film versus one that uses APS film. The strong point of APS is that you don't have to touch the film when loading or unloading. Drop in the film cartridge and the camera automatically unwinds and rewinds it. You also can switch—within a roll—from classic snapshot proportions (setting *C,* on the camera) to a somewhat wider image (*H*) or panorama (*P*) when you want it. APS cameras tend to be smaller and lighter than 35mm models, although either type of camera generally takes very good to excellent pictures.

Other features found on more expensive models of all cameras include an eyepiece with optical diopter adjustment, which lets you shoot without eyeglasses and weatherproofing for rainy days. Some models shoot underwater. An APS feature lets you swap film before a roll is finished, then reload the same roll later.

Digital Cameras

For those eager to replace a camera that shoots film, go digital. With their Liquid Crystal Display (LCD) screens, you can frame each shot exactly as you want it, shoot it, then take a look. If you don't like the scene, take it again. An indication of the popularity of digital cameras is that sales doubled from 2000 to 2001 and are expected to outstrip those of film cameras within a couple of years.

When peering at the plethora of digital cameras, what are the important areas? First is the pixel, or picture element. A pixel of less than 1 million now is substandard. Today's basic digital camera has two megapixels, which is good for quality 5″×7″ prints. For an 8″×10″ print, look at the two-megapixel models. Those who want still larger prints must consider a three- or four-megapixel model, and Minolta has a five-megapixel model. All of these cameras produce photos that can be scaled down to send via e-mail.

Most digital cameras are equipped with a 3X zoom lens, which is comparable to a 35–105mm film camera. A few have a 10X zoom lens.

How about memory cards that hold up to several hundred shots? Consider a USB cable to transfer your photos to your computer. Some use computer discs to hold high-resolution images, or a 156 MB compact disc with almost limitless storage capacity. CD-Rs and CD-RWs come with 650 MB of memory.

If you plan on printing your photos on an inkjet printer, use only the highest quality paper and ink so the photos will not fade quickly.

Know everything you wanted to know about buying a digital camera? Well, complexity is all part of the digital system. Or, as *Consumer Reports* observed in a review of digital cameras:

> To get the most out of any digital camera, you have to be prepared to spend time transferring images from camera to computer, and working with image-handling software. If you'd rather just drop off the film, then the digital may not be right for you.

Also, for several dollars, a processor can put photos on a CD when you bring in a roll for developing.

You can experiment with software to alter images, e-mail them, or post them on the Web. Your computer won't know that they started out as film.

Photographic Competition

Virtually every magazine that features unusual places to visit or whose subject is photography sponsors monthly or annual competitions.

Enter. The viewers do the choosing. Win an award for the quality of your work. You may not become famous for being chosen a winner once, but if photography is one of your present goals, entering the contests is a fine incentive for bringing the camera into your professional life.

CHAPTER FOUR

FOOD AND RECIPES
FOR THE WILD

Ah, What Food!

'Tis an ill cook that cannot lick his own
fingers.

—William Shakespeare (1564–1616)

One of the quiet joys of cooking over a campfire in
the wilderness after years of dining on food prepared in a sleek kitchen is that it opens a wonderful
way of enjoying yesterday. Sample a few recipes for
wilderness dishes from Horace Kephart's century-
old classic, *The Book of Camping and Woodcraft*,
and try your cooking skills at some of the great
dishes that have sustained generations of those who
love the wilderness.

His recipes begin with this advice before the
cook strikes a match: "Half of cookery is the fire

thereof. It is quite impossible to prepare a good meal over a higgledy-piggledy heap of smoking chunks, or over a fierce blaze, or over a great bed of coals that will warp cast-iron and melt everything else."

Be aware! A traditional dish for generations was a hearty Brunswick stew made with freshly shot squirrels appropriately skinned and cleaned. Today's campfire cooks can, if they are skilled with the trigger, bring some fresh squirrels to camp or substitute rabbit.

His recipe:

The ingredients needed, besides several squirrels [or rabbits], are:
1 qt. can tomatoes
1 pt. butter beans or limas
1 pt. green corn
6 potatoes, parboiled and sliced
1/2 lb. butter
1/2 lb. salt pork (fat)
1 teaspoonful black pepper
1/2 Cayenne
1 tablespoonful salt
2 tablespoonsful white sugar
1 onion minced, small
Soak the squirrels [or rabbits] half an hour in a gallon of cold, lightly salted water. Boil five minutes. Then put in the tomatoes, beans, corn, pork [cut into fine strips], potatoes, pepper, and squirrels [or rabbits].
Cover closely, and stew very slowly until potatoes are tender [about 45 minutes], stirring frequently to prevent burning. Remove potatoes. Add the sugar, and stew an hour longer. Then add the butter, cut into bits the size of a walnut and

roll in flour. Boil ten minutes. Then serve at once with potatoes on the side.

If you are using rabbit instead of wild squirrel, cook only until meat is tender.

Among Kephart's other recipes is cooking a fish before an open fire by planking. The technique is simple; the result, delicious.

Split and smooth a slab of sweet hardwood two or three inches thick, two feet long, and somewhat wider than the opened fish. Prop it in front of a bed of [hardwood] coals till it is sizzling hot. Split the fish down the back its entire length, but do not cut clear through the belly. Clean and wipe it quite dry. When plank is hot, spread fish out like an opened book, tack it, skin side down, to the planks and prop before fire. Baste continuously with a bit of pork on a switch held above it. Reverse ends of plank from time to time. If the flesh is flaky when pierced with a fork, it is done. Sprinkle salt and pepper over the fish, moisten with drippings, and serve on the hot plank. No better dish was ever set before an epicure.

To which, after planking one freshly caught two-pound trout, I can only add a solemn "Amen!"

Another technique that Kephart recommended for cooking rabbits, squirrels, chipmunks, or other small animals is to bake them in clay, which, he wrote,

hermetically seals the meat while cooking and better than baking in a kettle.

Draw the animal, but leave the skin and hair on. If it be a large bird, as a duck or goose, cut off

the head and most of the neck, also feet and pin-
ions, pull out tail feathers and cut tail off—to get
rid of the oil sac—but leave smaller feathers on.
If fish, do not scale. Moist and work some clay till
it is like softened putty. Roll it out in a sheet an
inch or two thick, and large enough to completely encase the animal. Cover the latter so
that no feather or hair projects. Place in fire and
cover with a good bed of coals and let it remain
with fire burning on top for about an hour, if a
fish or small bird. Larger animals require more
time, and had best be placed in a bake-hole over
night.

When done, break open the hard casing of
baked clay. The skin peels off with it, leaving the
meat perfectly clean and baked to perfection in
its own juices.

This method has been practiced for ages by the
gypsies and primitive peoples.

As for bread to go with a wilderness meal, don't
bring any from home. Instead, bake what Kephart
calls "army bread—Bannocks."

His recipe:

> 1 quart flour
> 1 teaspoon salt
> 1 tablespoon sugar
> 2 heaping teaspoonfuls baking powder

As this is made without grease, it is easier to
mix than biscuit dough. Mix the ingredients thoroughly and stir in enough cold water [about three
cups] to make a thick batter that will pour out
level. Mix rapidly with spoon until smooth and
pour at once into a Dutch oven or bake-pan. Bake
about 45 minutes or until no dough adheres to a
sliver stuck into the loaf.

Keeps fresh longer than yeast bread and does not dry out or mold. This is the kind of bread to bake when you are laying in a three-day's supply. It is more wholesome than biscuits, and is best eaten cold.

Preserved Foods

Now, try these historic recipes for sustenance on your next rafting, horse packing, or backpacking trip along wilderness trails. Explorers and Native Americans also may have dined on these recipes when traveling these same routes in generations past.

Pinole

Pinole was widely used in the southwestern United States and Mexico. Since the recipes were not ever really written down, try this one:

Ingredients:
1 quart of fresh corn, scraped off the cob
2 tablespoons brown sugar
Directions:
Place the corn kernels in a large open pot or cook in a 350° F oven until completely browned but not burned. Stir occasionally. Remove from heat and sprinkle with brown sugar. Continue cooking, stirring frequently, until kernels are completely coated with melted sugar. Remove from heat. Let stand until cool. In a grinder or blender, grind into a fine corn meal. At this point, the Indians would usually mix in scraps of dried or smoked meats or berries.

According to legend, when washed down with water, a handful would sustain a man on the trail for a day. How light can you travel?

Pemmican

Pemmican was adapted from Native American foods. From Mexico to the Arctic, it became a staple for generations of gold diggers, explorers, and fur traders. It can be eaten cold or mixed with flour and water and turned into a stew that explorers called "rubbadoo."

The basic recipe:

Ingredients:
Two pounds lean venison, buffalo, or beef, all fat removed, and cut into thin slices
1/2 pound lamb or beef fat
Directions:
Thoroughly dry the meat by hanging in the sun for several days, and cover at night to avoid dew. Or—modern style—hang from a dehydrator or a rack in an oven, with the door slightly ajar so the air can circulate, the heat coming only from the bottom, and the temperature at 110–130° F for 48 hours. Pound the fully dried meat by mortar and pestle, or grind in a blender, until it is powder. Chop the fat into small pieces, place in a pot of boiling water barely covering the fat, reduce to a simmer, and cook until all water has been boiled off. Separate the fat from any suet and let cool. Mix only the fat quickly with the ground meat and pack into airtight bags. Various nuts, ground fruits, and one teaspoon of sugar for every pound of dried meat may be added to the pemmican before packing it away.

Since exact proportions of melted fat to powdered meat was a choice of those who made it, vary proportions as you experiment with your own pemmican.

Jerky

Jerky also was adopted from Native Americans by Spanish explorers. The name itself is from the Spanish word *charqui,* for dried meat.

Ingredients:
3 pounds lean round steak
The cook's personal choice of one or more herbs, such as oregano, basil, thyme, cumin, coriander, and a hint of chili powder
Directions:
Trim all fat and muscle tissue from steak. Slice into thin strips 1/4-inch thick. Cut along the grain. Pound the spices into the meat firmly, but gently. Let stand at room temperature for eight hours. Dip the meat into very hot, but not boiling, water for 15 seconds. Hang the meat to dry under a hot sun for at least four full days. Cover at night to avoid dew. Or hang the meat on a rack in an oven with the door slightly ajar and a temperature of 120–130° F for 48 hours. When done, wrap tightly in plastic bags.

The jerky can be served "as is" and chewed on like a piece of flavored leather, or broken into small pieces and added to a vegetable soup, or made into a stew. Remember: Drying in an oven is only to remove moisture, not to cook the meat itself. Drying actually is best done in a commercial dehydrator.

Smoked Fish

Catch too many fish to eat in camp? Preserve them by smoking. Here's one time-honored method:

1. Cut off the heads, open from the belly, and clean thoroughly. Trim the outside as you wish.
2. Soak overnight in slightly salted water, then rinse.
3. Tie two sturdy cords, one six inches above the other, between two trees. Hang a tarp over the higher cord as you would if you were pitching it for a shelter, then stake the four corners to the ground, making a steeply sloping roof.
4. Hang the fish, butterfly fashion, on the lower cord.
5. Build a fire of hardwood scraps and branches directly under the center of the tarp. Keep the fire smoky, the thicker the better.
6. Smoke the fish for at least 24 hours.

The fish also can be hung in a bright sun one day, then smoked for 12 hours.

Drying Foods at Home

Mushrooms are simple to dry. In warm, sunny weather, tie small mushrooms to a string like pearls. Hang in direct sunlight for several days. Bring them in at night to avoid dew. For large mushrooms, cut off stems and slice into thin cooking strips. Spread the slices on a cooking screen and place in an oven between 110° and

120° F with the door slightly ajar. Keep in the oven for 12 to 24 hours, until thoroughly crisp. Dried mushrooms will keep for months. To rehydrate before cooking, soak dried mushrooms covered with warm water for 30 minutes. The mushroom water is tasty, as are the cooked mushrooms.

Other Foods

Both the oven- and sun-drying techniques are excellent for drying other foods you want to preserve at home. Tomatoes, peppers, onions, apples, shallots, as well as many other vegetables and fruits, can be home dried. The main preparation: Skim off peelings, remove seeds, and cut into thin slices. Dry in a modest oven about 120° F for 12–24 hours with the door slightly ajar, or in the sun for several days. Experiment. You be the judge.

For seniors curious about modern dehydrated recipes that go far beyond pemmican and pinole, one excellent publication is *Trail Food: Drying and Cooking Food for Backpackers and Paddlers* by Allan S. Kesselheim (McGraw-Hill).

Dining al Fresco

Cookery is become an art, a noble science.

—Robert Burton (1577–1640)

Dining well at any age, whether 18 or 81, is always a pleasure. It is even more so on an extended outdoor activity, whether you are backpacking for a week, paddling a canoe on a wilderness river, winter camping, or on a car camping adventure.

For weekend excursions, a few items out of the refrigerator enhanced by what you need at the nearest store is about as serious as most senior cooks are inclined to be when packing food for such a short adventure. But when the trips grow longer, and especially when they involve several people, both planning menus and quantities are of far greater importance.

You like chili made from freshly ground beef when you are four days on the trail? How about substituting ground canned corned beef? Remember that wonderful paella you devoured on a sunny beach years ago on your unforgettable trip to Buenos Aires? Replace the fresh shrimp with canned shrimp, and the same goes for the chicken. Turn a package of dehydrated chicken soup into a tasty Chinese soup with soy sauce, grated fresh ginger, and the shiitake mushrooms you dehydrated at home.

You understand!

Basic Meals

Breakfasts

This is a combination of familiar quick-energy carbohydrates, proteins, and fats that continue to feed the energy furnace many hours later.

Hot instant cereals, such as oatmeal or Cream of Wheat, are popular. They can be quickly prepared by covering with boiling water. You can add minced dry fruit to the water and simmer for ten minutes before pouring it on cereal. Although cold cereals are welcome, select nutritious brands and avoid those that are highly sugared.

Whole freeze-dried eggs replace the fresh. Vary pancakes, some made with flour, some with potato (latkes). Serve with syrup or applesauce. There is almost no limit on the canned ham, bacon, salami, and sausages—some which can stay edible for weeks without refrigeration—available for the hungry at breakfast. Instant coffee is quicker, and less time consuming, than making it fresh.

Lunches

Medium and hard cheeses, peanut butter and jelly, crackers or firm breads, canned fish such as tuna, salmon, or sardines, dried fruits, sun-dried vegetables, GORP or trail mix, and powdered drink mixes are all welcome. But always have fresh water on hand—if necessary, bring your own water filter. On a chilly day, try cups of instant Japanese soups, made with boiling water, which are available at most supermarkets these days.

A handful of GORP is popular for midday nibbling.

Dinner

We have one absolute on all my trips, whether in summer or winter: Every dinner begins with at least 12 ounces of soup per person. Since the body consumes water all day long, which usually is not sufficiently replaced while active, a hearty soup helps make up for the loss of body fluid.

Consider what else goes into your dinners at home that you enjoy, and bring them. Starches can be of the instant variety, which markedly shortens the cooking time, including, but by no means limited to, rice, couscous, mashed potatoes, pastas, and noodles. Firm breads are tasty.

An endless variety of hearty dishes can be made using freeze-dried and canned meats, fish, chicken, and vegetables. Long-lasting fresh vegetables, such as carrots and celery, taste wonderful a week later, and "store boughten" pastries that withstand rough handling are welcome for desert.

A pleasant wine is always welcome at any dinner I've enjoyed with seniors, whether at home or on a distant waterway.

Fish

Freshly caught fish from river, stream, or lake is welcome to enhance any meal. But on my trips, we have one policy for those who grab a few minutes to toss out a fish hook: What you catch we eat, or you toss it back after someone takes a picture of a grinning fisherwoman holding her prize aloft.

How many calories do you anticipate each person on a trip for whom you are making up the menus will eat? The general diet for active adults is about 2,000 calories a day at home. Add another 1,000 for seniors engaged in such activities as trail hiking, bicycling, and paddling in the out-of-doors. Add 500 more when off on winter joys.

Figuring portions and calories is a longwinded and laborious chore. It will save massive amounts of figuring, however, to use the caloric value of foods in the Sierra Club totebook, *Food for Knapsackers and Other Trail Travellers,* by Hasse Bunnelle.

Figure 4.1   Sierra Club Chart

Food	Ounces per person per day	Calories	Comments
Breakfast			
Dried fruits	1.5	110	Excellent when eaten dry, mixed with cereal or simmered.
Cereals; compact cold cereals such as various granolas, Familia, Grape Nuts, etc.	1.5	150–180	Avoid presugared cereals, or cereals with high sugar content. Sugars add bulk without adding nutritional value.
Instant hot cereals: Quaker Oats, Wheatena, Cream of Wheat, etc.	1.5	150	Some are prepared by simply adding hot water, others must be boiled for a minute or two. Cereals with such extras as raisins, fruits, or flavorings are especially popular. If the cereal does not contain any, add them yourself. (Note: Cereals commercially packaged into individual servings usually contain portions too small for husky camp appetites. Figure on one and one-half packages per person.)
Bacon, Spam	1.4	250–300	For long trips buy the canned varieties. Use the grease for cooking.
Boneless ham or shoulder	1.4	160	Take precooked only.
Eggs	two per person	170	Whether fresh, freeze-dried, or dehydrated, eggs are a breakfast staple.
Potatoes, dehydrated and prepackaged	1.0	150–200	Available in supermarkets; exceptionally popular.
Pancake mixes	2.0	200	Popular, but drags out a breakfast. Reserve for days when you'll be in camp.
Lunch			
Crackers, such as RyKrisp	1.5	175	Keep well and are excellent with peanut butter and jelly.

(continued)

Figure 4.1 *(continued)*

Food	Ounces per person per day	Calories	Comments
Lunch (continued)			
Firm "German" or Westphalian pumpernickel	1.5	100	Also keeps well, but is more likely to be crushed than firm crackers.
Various dry salamis and bolognas	1.5	120–150	Many varieties keep well without refrigeration.
Cheeses	1.5	170	Look for hard cheeses (such as Monterey jack, Swiss, or provolone) or those canned cheeses that do not need refrigeration. On shorter trips try the canned French cheeses such as Brie and Camembert. Avoid cheeses with unusual and strong flavors.
Tuna fish, salmon, sardines	1.5	125	Canned tuna can be served as is, or mixed with mayonnaise or sandwich spread.
Deviled meats	1.5	Varies	Sample at home; some types are quite spicy.
Gorp	1.0	220	Use salted nuts or salted soybeans when mixing gorp, especially in hot weather.
Nuts, various	1.0	1.75	
Peanut butter	1.0	200	A luncheon favorite.
Jelly	0.3	80	To add a touch of something special to the peanut butter.
Candy	0.5	75	Avoid candy that melts.
Dried fruits	1.3	100	Raisins and apples are the most popular.
Powdered drink mixes, including instant ice coffee and tea		Varies	The label will give you the approximate amount per cupful.
Dinner			
Soup, dehydrated	Varies	Check on label.	Packaged soups specify the servings in either 6- or 8-ounce amounts. Figure on 12 liquid ounces per person.
Sauces and gravy mixes	Varies	Check on label.	Usually a package makes an 8-ounce cupful. Popular with

Figure 4.1   *(continued)*

Food	Ounces per person per day	Calories	Comments
Dinner (continued)			
			almost every starch dish from mashed potatoes to couscous.
Meat, fresh—steak, boneless	5.0	250	A fine main course the first night in camp.
Fowl, fresh—chicken, turkey	16.0	140	Chickens broil in about 40 minutes; turkey takes much longer. Also best the first night at your put-in.
Canned corned beef			
Canned roast beef	3.0	200	
Canned ham, boneless	3.0	230	For large groups, buy the meat in No. 10 cans. Quantities and servings are usually clearly specified and accurate.
Canned chicken, turkey	3.0	220	
Canned tuna	3.0	250	
Freeze-dried beef, chops, patties	1.0	130	
Pasta, noodles	3.0	300	
Precooked rice	2.0	200	
Dehydrated mashed potatoes	1.6	160	
Dehydrated potato dishes, such as au gratin or scalloped		210	Servings specified on the label are about 50% less than hungry adults will eat in camp.
Couscous, kasha		160	Serve with a light gravy mix.
Desserts: Jell-O, instant pudding, instant cheesecake, etc.			
Staples			
Coffee, instant	0.15`	0	
Tea, instant		0	
Tea bags	2 bags	0	
Hot chocolate mix	1.0	150	
Nonfat dry milk			
Flour or biscuit mix		100	Buy in prepackaged 1-quart envelopes; figure on 1½

(continued)

Figure 4.1 *(continued)*

Food	Ounces per person per day	Calories	Comments
Staples (continued)			
Flour or biscuit mix (cont.)			quarts per day per four people. The box will indicate the number of biscuits its contents will make; judge accordingly. Mixes also can be used for thickening instead of ordinary flour.
Sugar	1.0	100	An artificial sweetener will substantially reduce the amount of sugar bulk you must carry.
Dehydrated soup greens	0.1		For enriching many dishes.
Dehydrated onion flakes	0.1		For enriching many dishes.
Dried mushrooms	0.15		Buy dried Chinese mushrooms.
Margarine	Varies	230	Read the label; some require no refrigeration and will keep for several weeks.
*Condiments**			
Salt			
Pepper			
Basil			
Thyme			
Oregano			
Chili powder			
Curry powder			
Ginger, powdered			
Tarragon			
Cloves			
Red pepper			
Sesame seed			
Chervil			
Parsley			
Bouillon cubes			
Garlic or garlic powder			
Rosemary			
Cumin			
Marjoram			
Cinnamon			
Maple flavoring			Useful if you make your own syrup out of sugar.

*Plus any others your recipes call for.

In another Sierra Club totebook, *Cooking for Camp and Trail,* the authors note:

> Carefully planned diets contain sufficient quantities of vitamins and minerals for most people, but because cooking destroys vitamin C, supplements of that are advisable on any trip more than a few days long. If there is any question about the nutritional content of your canned or dried foods, add vitamin and mineral supplements.

GORP

What else besides raisins and peanuts?

—Anonymous

For a hundred or maybe two hundred years or more, GORP has been the ultimate trail nosh. The gourmet of hiking snacks.

The most intensive research into where and why it came into being has produced little more than it was developed because mouths on early New England trails often developed the need for a bit of a bite between breakfast and lunch, and again between lunch and dinner. Thus, GORP came into being.

The initials, so say unknown voices, have long insisted they stand for "Good Old Raisins and Peanuts." Be that as it may, the original formula has grown by leaping from plain old peanuts to chocolate-covered peanuts, and from ordinary raisins to crumbled raisin cookies, and has added handfuls of these and clusters of those. Be inventive. Be creative. Make your own GORP. And, withal, add what you will to your own recipe that is healthy as well as tasty when snacking while hiking the greater divide.

Oh, yes. Please drop a sample in a plastic bag and mail it to me. Why, I may use your recipe in my next outdoor tome. With credit, of course.

The Search for Wild Foods

I know a bank whereon the wild thyme blows.
Where oxlips and nodding violet grows
Quite over-canopied with luscious woodbine,
With sweet musk-roses and with eglantine.

—William Shakespeare,
A Midsummer Night's Dream

For seniors aware of the never-ending need to keep physically active at any age, whether you are a newly retired 60 or an aging 90, few might consider stalking across fields and plains, trekking through forests, or climbing mountains for wild edibles as an enjoyable exercise that keeps the muscles moving and the mind alert. But it actually is. Of course, it's essential to know that what you actually are searching for is a specific wild, edible plant and to appreciate the pleasure of eating a food fresher than the freshest, untouched and unsullied by a human hand.

Before searching for delicious wild foods, first pursue several of the excellent books that deal with the wild and edible. Among those I recommend are:

Stalking the Wild Asparagus, published and written by Euell Gibbons

Mushrooms and Other Fungi: Their Form and Colour, H. Kleijn (Doubleday)

Edible Wild Plants of Eastern North America, revised by Reed C. Rollins (Harper & Row)

Now, open the pages and devour what you are going to find.

Both the outer bark and the cambium layer (inner bark) of the ordinary pine tree (*Pinus*) are rich in Vitamin C and can be nibbled on, raw or cooked. Native Americans and early pioneers regularly gathered the cambium layer to dry and grind up. The settlers used it as flour. Pine needles from young branches are pleasant tasting both raw and in tea, but eat sparingly: They can lead to diarrhea.

The seeds of pinon pine (*Pinaceae*) cones, a low-growing conifer in the western United States, are a special treat. Char the cones in a low fire to loosen the seeds. The nuts of the pinon pine tree are also a delicacy. The trouble is getting the nuts out of the pine cones. Try a hammer or a good size piece of rock to loosen them. Lightly pan fry or roast the nuts.

Cactus is found in almost every sunny place. Cut off the fleshy stems, peel off the skin, and have a nutritious raw treat.

The blue berries found on juniper trees (*Juniperus*) are nutritious but somewhat bitter when eaten raw. To cook, pound them in a mortar and pestle, then boil. Now, dine.

Ordinary sweet birch trees (*Betula lenta*) are the lost wanderer's friend. The inner cambium layer is edible raw or cooked, but note that heavy cutting of the cambium layer will kill a tree. To sample, cut small pieces only. The outer bark may be peeled and crumbled for a fire starter. The bark also may be peeled into sheets that can be formed into plates or large pots or even to cover holes in your wigwam.

Nature's Supermarket

The supermarket of the wilderness is the cat-tail (*Typha latifolia*). The first tiny shoots in the spring are edible raw. As they grow into sprigs 10 to 12 inches long, they can be peeled and boiled like asparagus. The tangled roots can be eaten raw, boiled, baked, or roasted. At the end of the roots are tiny bulbs that will sprout into new cat-tails next spring. These are savory. Peel and eat them. The brownish spikes that appear in the late summer and fall can be used as natural decoration for your home or apartment. When the yellow flower spikes finally appear, they can be husked, then boiled and eaten with butter. Next, the spikes swell with yellow pollen. Shake the pollen into a pan and carry it back to camp. Mix 1 part pollen with 3 parts flour when making pancakes or muffins.

Don't ignore the arrow-shaped leaves of the arrowhead (*Saggitaria*), which is found along the edge of streams and swamps. The leaf may lie flat or wave to you in the air. Dig under the plant for the edible small tubers on the roots. Boil or bake these like potatoes.

It's cheaper to find some table delights in the wilds than in the grocery store. For example, watercress (*Nasturtium officinale*) looks the same growing in freshwater springs as it does in the vegetable rack. And the uncurled fiddleheads of bracken fern (*Peridium*), which is rather coarse and covered with hairy felt at the base, is yours for free when found in the woods.

Migrating Foods

Purslane (*Portulaca oleracea*) migrated from India to our western continent. This ground-hugging plant is rarely more than two inches high but can grow a foot across. The stems, leaves, and flowers are edible and are popular in salads, soups, and stews.

If the ancient commentary that "giant oaks from tiny acorns grow" tempts you to munch on them, here's the technique for enjoying oak (*Quercus*) acorns that was used by Indians: Pound the acorns into flour, then leach it thoroughly to remove the tannic acid.

In the spring, it's sheer folly to jerk out the dandelions (*Taraxacum*) sprouting on your lawn and toss them away. The fresh young leaves are succulent in salad as well as a source of nutrients. Dried dandelion roots as well as elderberries also make a nutritious (if not delicious) tea, and some people still make dandelion wine.

In their journals, Lewis and Clark reported that the Indians in western Montana dried sunflower seeds (*Helianthus*), then pounded them into a fine powder. "Sometimes they add a portion of water and drink it thus diluted."

You needn't walk far to discover plantain (*Plantago*). My mother used to tear it out of the garden as a pernicious weed. Now, its young leaves are a pleasure in my salads.

A Pioneer Food

Once known as groundnuts, Indian potatoes (*Apios americana*) were one of the first wild foods eaten by the earliest settlers. In 1590, Thomas Hariot wrote that they were "a kind of roots of round forme, some of the bigness of walnuts, some far greater, which are found in moist and marsh grounds, growing one by another in ropes, or as though they were fastened with a string, being boiled or sodden they were very good meate."

Most berries are a pleasure to discover, especially when you are huffing and puffing along portage trails where bushes loaded with a tasty berry are a superb excuse to stop carrying and start nibbling. Blackberries and dewberries are among the most common and tasty wild berries in the nation. The usual way of distinguishing the berries is that blackberries are borne on upright canes and those plucked from trailing vines are dewberries. Serviceberries are a popular nibble-and-enjoy treat along the western regions of Canada and the United States. Along a wide span of the east, the juneberry, also known as the shadberry, is a hiker's pleasure. Although not especially sought for its flavor, the elderberry is noted for another great use: making wine. One recipe:

20 pounds of elderberries
5 quarts boiling water
10 cups sugar

Mash the elderberries into a five-gallon crock, add the boiling water, then cover and let stand for three days. Strain the juice through cheesecloth and return to the crock. Add the sugar and let it stand in the covered crock until fermentation ceases. Remove the scum, pour into bottles, and tightly cork. It should not be sipped for at least a year.

Warning: If a berry is an unknown, beware. Some are quite bitter and others are poisonous.

For Something Sweet

Tiny wild strawberries are far sweeter than those found in the stores.

A wide variety of mushrooms are found in woodlands and on plains. Know those you will pluck and eat. For positive identification, carry a mushroom book that shows the mushrooms in natural colors and where they grow. Never forget that there are three—the fly mushroom, the *Panther amanita,* and the destroying angel—which are killers.

Survival

The search for edibles is not only to find delights for the table, but also can mean survival if something goes wrong in the wilderness. Here is one example:

> Lone Man Lost in Woods
> Lives off Lily Pad Roots
> Minneapolis, May 24 (AP)—A 69-year-old North Dakota man survived on lily pad roots for eight days after becoming lost in the dense woods

of Minnesota's remote Northwest Angle before a couple found him along a road late Saturday.

The man, John C. Johnson of Pembina, N.D., was taken to a hospital in Roseau, Minn., an hour south of the Angle which extends from Manitoba into Lake of the Woods, about 350 miles north of Minneapolis. The area, which is not contiguous with the rest of the state, is accessible by road through Canada or by boat across the lake.

Mr. Johnson endured heavy rainstorms and temperatures as low as 40 degrees at night, clad only in blue jeans, a short sleeved shirt, baseball cap, red suspenders and running shoes.

"He told me he probably ate 12 lily pad roots during the eight days," said his daughter, Jolene Windt of Kokomo, Ind. She said he kept warm by huddling in hollow stumps and covering himself with bark (*New York Times,* May 25, 1998).

Scouting the Natural Proteins

The swamps, plains, and farm regions are lands of plenty for the proteins we need for healthy survival. During an old war, the military taught pilots a secret to staying alive if they were shot down: Dine silently on such proteins as katydids, locusts, grasshoppers, and crickets. First remove the wings and, if you are fussy, nip off the heads.

It's not necessary for today's senior campers to creep secretly in the grass to find grubs, worms, and caterpillars for a camp meal. Avoid those with hair or fuzz, which may indicate that they are slightly poisonous.

For a rare meat: Catch a snake, any snake. If it is poisonous, the poison is in the mouth, so cut off its head. Open the body and clean out the guts. Remove the skin, if you are finicky, and broil!

All species of ants, from tiny red to large carpenter, were widely used by Indians, especially in the Southwest. They would first roast them, then grind them into powder that they would add to a stew cooking over the fire.

Among the delights that are found in freshwater streams and ponds throughout the country, and are easy to catch, are crayfish (*Cambarus*), also known as crawdads and freshwater crabs. They look like miniature lobsters. Sometimes they can be found hiding under smaller rocks near the shore, but mostly they thrive in deeper, quiet water. Catch crayfish with a piece of bacon. The technique is simple: Tie a small chunk of bacon with a piece of metal on a long string fastened to the end of a pole. (Note: Do not use lead fishing weights, which poison the water.) Toss in the bait, wait a few minutes, and slowly pull the little goodie ashore. The quickest way to satisfy hunger is to toss them into boiling water. They will turn from grayish to bright red. Remove and dine on the meat in the tail, which is as succulent as lobster.

Gourmet Food—At Home

Turtles and terrapins usually are thought of as gourmet food in a fine restaurant, but you can have them in your own house tonight by capturing them after the healthy effort of tramping through the areas where they live. Search slow moving streams, ponds, and marshy water. Terrapins may be caught by special hooks, but are easy to catch by hand when you spot them while wading through the shallow waters where they thrive. Snapping turtles are generally grabbed by the tail while they are waddling in damp, shady groves. Hold your prize upside own, chop its head off, and let it hang by the tail to bleed before cutting him up for dinner.

To prepare turtles, scrub thoroughly in clean water after cutting off the head, lay it on its back, cut off the bottom shell, and remove the lungs, intestines, and internal organs, especially the gall bladder, a green bag on the left side. Clean thoroughly again. A basic way of getting the meat is to cover the turtle with water, then boil it until the meat slips from the bones. Use the meat in a soup or stew.

Frog legs are another expensive delicacy at elegant restaurants. Catch your own. The finest are the giant bullfrog (*R. catesbeiana*). They are most easily caught at night in shallow ponds when spotted by a flashlight. One method is to use a long bamboo pole with a trident spear on the end to spear them. Some frog hunters use a net on the end of a long pole. Cut off the back legs, which are almost the entire frog, and skin and clean them before cooking.

So, you seniors who are curious about wild stalks, dining on turtle or on frog legs, or making your wine from a berry or root, go and search. Your search may involve a lot of wilderness tramping, but it's a healthy activity, and each trip ends, as it must, with something special you have gathered for the table.

CHAPTER FIVE

CONSERVATION

> Conservation is a state of harmony between
> men and land.

> —Aldo Leopold (1886–1948)

"Conservation" is a rich and pleasing word that rolls easily off the tongue. The older outdoor wanderers who identify themselves as conservationists imply not only that they acquired a great love of life beyond street and shopping malls during years of roaming mountain and desert but also acquired a substantial understanding of what must be done to preserve and protect our natural resources and all forms of life therein.

However, being a "worthy conservationist" also is more than simply possessing knowledge. It also requires getting involved on some level of activity supporting conservation organizations.

Seniors, including those who have always been fulfilled by trekking or paddling the great outdoors but whose age and physical skills no longer let them swing freely off into the wilderness as they once did, may still help out in outdoor conservation projects.

There also are many non-physically stressful conservation activities in which they can put their beliefs in conservation to work. Consider some of these:

1. When issues arise regarding conservation projects in your neighborhood, attend public meetings called by local or state officials to discuss them.
2. Ask specific questions and urge public answers.
3. Write letters to the editor expressing your conservation views. Editors are genuinely interested in issues of local importance. Not only is it likely that your letter will be published, but you can also show copies of your letter to both friends and public officials.
4. Express your views on local radio stations with call-in hosts.
5. If you feel a conservation project would merit support as a television feature on the local news, suggest it to the local stations.
6. Write to your senators and representative by name to oppose or support specific legislation. Be certain to list the legislative code number of any bill in which you are interested.

7. Join one or all of the following organizations that play a critical role in conservation on the local, national, and international levels:

Adirondack Mountain Club, 814 Doggins Road, Lake George, NY 12845, 518-668-3746, www.adk.org

Alpine Club of Canada, P.O. Box 8040, Indian Flats Road, Canmore, Alberta T1W 2T8, 403-762-4481

American Hiking Society, P.O. Box 20160, Washington, D.C. 20041-2160, 202-301-6714

American Canoe Association, 7432 Alban Station Blvd., Suite B-232, Springfield, VA 22150, 703-451-0141

American Rivers, Inc., 1025 Vermont Ave., N.W., Suite 720, Washington, D.C. 20005, 202-347-9224

American Water Resources Association, 4 West Federal Street, Middleburg, VA 20118, info@awra.org, ph: 540-687-8390, fax: 540-687-8395

Appalachian Mountain Club, 5 Joy Street, Boston, MA 02108, 617-523-0722, www.outdoors.org

Appalachian Trail Conference, P.O. Box 807, Harpers Ferry, WV 25425, 304-535-6331

Defenders of Wildlife, 1101 14th Street, N.W., Washington, D.C. 20005, 202-682-9400

Environmental Defense Fund, 25 Park Ave. South, New York, NY 10010, 212-505-2100

The Mountaineers, 300 Third Ave. West, Seattle, WA 98119, 206-284-6310

The National Audubon Society, 700 Broadway, New York, NY 10022, 212-979-3000

The Nature Conservancy, 1815 North Lynn Street, Arlington, VA 22209, 703-841-5300

National Wildlife Federation, 1400 16th Street, Washington, D.C. 20036, 202-797-6800

New England Trail Conference, P.O. Box 145, Weston, VT 05161

Pacific Crest Trail Association, P.O. Box 1048, Seattle, WA 98111

Professional Paddlesports Association, 7432 Alban Station Blvd., Suite A-111, Springfield, VA 22150, 703-451-3864

Rails-to-Trail Conservancy, 1400 16th Street, N.W., Suite 300, Washington, D.C. 20036, 202-797-5400; www.railtrails.org. By 2002, Rails-to-Trail had converted more than 12,000 miles of abandoned railroad tracks into walking-hiking-biking trails.

Sierra Club, 85 Second Street, San Francisco, CA 94105, 415-776-2211, www.sierraclub .org. The Sierra Club is the largest outdoor and conservation-oriented organization in the United States.

The Wilderness Society, 1615 M Street, N.W., Washington, D.C. 20036, 1-800-THE-WILD

The Wildlife Society, 5410 Grosvenor Lane, Bethesda, MD 20814, 301-897-9770

Hold up. We're not through yet. There is not a state or local chapter of a national outdoor society that is not involved in service projects. These may range from building a new trail to cleaning up abused campsites. Check the local headquarters of state and national parks and forests. They always can put to use whatever muscle you can provide to clean up or build an outdoor facility.

Get your hands muddy. Put on lots of suntan lotion. Hammer a nail or two. But put your conservationist philosophy to work in speech, in print, or with muscle and sweat. Out beyond!

You're never too old.

Low-Impact Camping

In God's wildness lies the hope of the world—
the great, fresh, unblighted, unredeemed
wilderness.

—John Muir (1838–1914)

As a kid living in the shadows of the towering Bannock range peaks that surround Pocatello, Idaho, my great joy was when good ol' Boy Scout Troop 7 set off on a long weekend trek beyond sagebrush fields and into the birch and pine forests that flourish thousands of feet above the valley. Loaded with all the weight we could carry, off we started.

Our scoutmaster set a pace we all considered too damn fast, but he did stop occasionally for a few minutes' rest. Packs on the ground, we moaned and grunted about how far we'd walked, and guessed at how much further it would be to reach our camp site.

"He don't have to walk so damn fast."

"Yeah. He's got long legs."

"Oh, okay," said the scoutmaster. "I hear yuh. Let's go."

On went the packs, and they didn't come off again until we arrived at his chosen camping area for this particular hike—a clearing several acres across with a beautiful stream slicing through it and sparkling in the sun. Our scoutmaster held up his hand. Then he bellowed, "Patrols. Pick out your own campsite. Get the tents up. Pick out a fire site. Okay, guys, let's go."

For three days we set up our sites as veteran campers, dug ditches for our tents, and built patrol fires, one for each patrol to cook on. To prove our skill as veterans of the wild woods, we chopped down branches, then built a six-foot bridge across the stream and a six-foot-high signal tower strong enough to support the weight of one boy.

Before we left, we cleaned up the area. We left the bridge and tower standing, of course. We piled leftover wood by the three fire sites. All ashes had been carefully sprinkled to assure no spark was alive. All leftover food and debris were buried in deep holes. Looking at the site as we started for home I still remember a dozen pine trees stripped of their branch tips, which we had used as mattresses in our tents, and the stumps of the trees we had hacked down to build the bridge and tower, and the ditching left around the tent sites.

"A fine job," our scoutmaster told us. "Look how neat and clean everything is."

Of course, within an hour animals would dig up the buried food, but that was not our concern. In the 1930s, as every senior camper today knows, that was the way the nation camped. Your most important tool was that sharp hatchet hanging from your hip, and you didn't bother with tearing down what it had built while you were there.

So, we do it differently today. Now we protect, not destroy. Now we gather only branches lying on the ground for a camp fire, or we cook over a portable gas stove. We don't ditch tents. What garbage cannot be burned, we pack out with us in plastic bags. The fire pit, if there is one, is filled in and covered with dirt and leaves.

The theme today: Take nothing but photos. Leave nothing but footprints. And cover the hole where you cooked.

Where you make camp is largely determined by your method of travel and where you are travelling. Consider: If you are paddling a remote wilderness river or lake, or hiking a seldom traveled forest trail, wherever there is enough open space for the tents is where you make a camp.

On the other hand, it is increasingly likely that however you travel, whether canoeing, backpacking, bicycling, or in a SUV, in all state or national parks or forests, camping is restricted to specific locations. Not always a bad choice for seniors, because the sites often have camp areas with fireplaces, often have picnic tables, and many also include open-front Adirondack lodges.

Regardless of your method of travel or whether you're alone or with a group, there are practices that every camper, from a boy scout to an 80-plus senior, should practice—and support—today.

1. When possible, camp where others have camped before. The first sign of this is an old fire pit. Put it to use if you are cooking over an open fire.
2. Pitch your tent where others have pitched theirs. Leave the green and grassy places untouched. After all, you did bring a comfortable

sleeping pad to protect your shoulders and butt from the hard ground.

3. When setting up camp in an untouched area, treat it gently. Locate the general camp site at a reasonable distance from the nearest stream or lake.

4. If you have to dig a hole for a new fire pit, save the dirt and ground detritus to shovel back on the site before hiking off.

Outdoor Bathrooms

Toilets are a wilderness problem. Of course, you can walk anywhere and go behind a tree—as long as it is at least 200 feet from water. That's fine for urinating. But what about taking a shit in the woods, and what about the toilet paper? One small shovel for a small group is excellent. Bury the feces and the toilet paper in a small hole and cover it up when you are through. Some ardent purists insist the used toilet paper should be burned or stuffed into the plastic bag for garbage which you take out with you. And there are those who would abolish toilet paper and recommend clean stone or leaves in summer and snow balls in the winter. Dr. Wade Johnson, the New York City internist with a large senior practice, was aghast at this suggestion. He warned firmly that the anus could become infected from dirty stones or leaves, or smeared with painful toxins from inadvertently using leaves from poison ivy or poison sumac. As for snowballs? "Brrrrrrr."

Problems

In an area infested with mosquitoes, locate the tents where they can be brushed by the prevailing breeze. Even a light breeze will help sweep the little buggers away. Praise the sight of bats. They gobble mosquitoes by the thousands.

However, be cautious about camping completely in the open. On one Sierra Club canoe trip in northern Quebec, our first night's camp was on an open, wide bluff overlooking the river. About 100 feet back was a heavy growth of pine. Three tents—two sturdy double-wall self-erecting tents and one A-frame—were completely in the open. Another was partially under the pines.

A storm swept in violently at about 2 A.M. Bolts of lightning. Slashing rain. The scene in the open area was bedlam. The A-frame tent was blown over. Tents flapped wildly in the wind, but the tent partially protected from the wind suffered no damage. The next night's camp was on another island with most of the trees on one side. The lesson of last night was remarkably apparent. All the tents were under partial protection from wild winds by the trees.

Pitch your own tent in a place with natural drainage so that an unexpected rain will not come flooding in. Unlike the canvas tents that campers once used, which leaked water if you touched the sides during a rain storm—World War II vets slept in them—today, no way. Modern tent fabrics are lightweight and genuinely waterproof. All self-supporting, double-wall tents have flooring, but the flooring can become damp in a heavy rain. The seams of all tents, however well-designed, should be resealed annually to prevent leakage in a heavy storm. In addition, it's a clever idea to have a sheet of plastic slightly larger than the tent that can be pitched under the tent.

Roll up the edges and slip them under the bottom of the tent flooring to help keep the interior dry.

A tarp is a welcome necessity for a group. Even the 79-year-old appreciates that she can sit under it to keep out of the brilliant sun or dine under it to avoid a drenching rain. My preference is long staple Egyptian cotton with built-in grommets and ties. Square foot for square foot, this particular tarp is lighter than plastic and can be packed into a smaller space.

Putting up a tarp is easy. Tie it to nearby trees. Today we use nails only in an emergency. You can toss a tarp over a single rope tied to two trees as a ridge pole, then tie the corners to spikes in the ground. Or you can carry an aluminum pole, which can hold up the center of the tarp, and tie the four corners to other trees or to ground spikes.

Pitch tents upwind from the cooking area. Since campers have a pleasant habit of strolling back and forth between tents, keep the cooking area out of their line of travel, and keep them out of the cooking area by setting a table aside with snacks: maybe a couple beers, or a salad, or potato chips. The unquestioned law of the cooking area: Cooks only!

Wheels in the Wilderness

When prowling the wilderness, whether by foot, bicycle, motorcycle, llama, or SUV, stay on the existing roads and trails. This is equally true for hikers who cut straight across trails specifically designed in a switchback style to prevent erosion, or 80-year olds driving an SUV across open areas to prove their SUV can cut off a mile or two of road while tearing the hell out of an ancient swamp.

Hey, we all have an obligation to protect, not rip apart, even a corner of an ancient trail. Save it for our great-grandchildren.

Dogs in Camp

The one absolutely unselfish friend that man can have in this selfish world, the one that never deserts him, the one that never proves ungrateful or treacherous, is his dog. When all other friends desert, he remains.

—George Vest, Senate speech (1830–1904)

We had just finished pitching our tent in a corner of a campsite on an island for canoeists, kayakers, and rafters when I heard a couple of dogs barking. Most unusual, I thought, for a campground that could be reached only by boat to permit dogs.

I looked over as an elderly man with a white beard blowing in the wind walked past with the two small mixed-breed dogs on short leashes.

We nodded. "I didn't know you could bring dogs to this campsite," I said.

"Oh, you've got to get permission first. They wanna make sure dogs are inoculated." He grinned. His dogs barked in unison. "Yeah, they are noisy, aren't they? But," he assured me, "they won't be noisy when they're sleeping on my feet tonight."

"Don't you find it a problem to have dogs camping?"

"Well," he hesitated, "not really. Of course, you've got to take special care with them." "I realize that," I said. "I've never taken a dog camping. On my next trip ours will be coming with me."

Our conversation focused on what is involved when dogs tag along on a camping, canoeing, or trail trip. We agreed that many older campers, whose kids have long grown and moved on, are eager to take their pets with them but, if they do, they must be aware of the problems involved as well as the tail-wagging pleasures of petting their dog in front of a campfire at night.

Basic Requirements

Seniors who are enthusiastic about having their faithful Fido with them must look first at some basic requirements. For example, most camp areas and motels that permit dogs insist they must remain on a leash. Many require that you have proof of rabies inoculation. If, perchance, your dog takes a nip out of an unsuspecting hand, he may have his head removed and rushed to a laboratory for examination if you don't have proof of inoculation. Both a health certificate and proof of inoculation are required for dogs entering Canada and Mexico.

When driving anywhere, make certain that your dog always wears a metal identification tag in case he slips away without notifying you first. Make frequent stops to give the dog a chance to pee, stretch, and drink water.

The Gaines Company, which produces animal food, also recommends that in a car or tent, a pet needs reassurances from the people she knows and loves, and will find comfort in a familiar toy or even her regular food dish.

Preconditioning a Household Pet

If the dog leaping joyfully about the gear on the living room floor is going on a backpacking trip with her master but is only accustomed to chasing a ball on a rug in the house, then she should be preconditioned to more vigorous overland travel. Veterinarians recommend daily walks of several miles with your dog through wooded parks and on rocky trails for at least two weeks before she leaps joyfully into the family car.

In the woodlands, examine your dog every night for ticks. The immediate treatment is to pull out the ticks with tweezers and cover the spot with a dab of antibiotic ointment. Cut away burrs in and around the ears and feet.

Generally, dog first aid consists of treating wounds from another dog or small animal. Wash any small wound with a solution of Epsom salts. She'll lick the wound clean if she can reach it. Dogs rarely get bitten by snakes, but should this happen, there is virtually nothing that can be done except to keep the dog quiet and seek immediate veterinary attention. Either she will survive or she won't.

A dog new to the woodlands will tangle only once with a porcupine. Unless the quills are deeply imbedded, pull them out of her cheeks, nose, and mouth by hand. Do not let the barbs work their way into her body. If they do, the dog must be taken as quickly as possible to a vet.

What's That Smell?

No one needs to explain to the master what that terrible smell is that has suddenly come upon the dog. I have been advised that washing a dog with vinegar or tomato juice will reduce the odor a skunk leaves when it raises its tail. This is not necessarily true, although it helps. But do not wash her down with a detergent containing bleach. If you have a dog chain—not a leather leash, which she can chew through—spray her with a pleasing professional deodorizer then tie her upwind from the camp until the skunk delight dissipates.

On the trail, a dog can carry her food and a collapsible bowl, not to exceed one-quarter of her own weight, in a dog pannier, according to Mike Yerkes, director of Urban Programs and Outdoor Leadership with the Appalachian Mountain Club. He recommends feeding a dog food that is as similar as possible to the same food she eats at home.

If you are traveling by boat, the pannier can be filled with plastic ping-pong balls to serve as a life preserver should she fall overboard or leap out to chase a moose standing by the shore.

According to Dr. Chuck Hibler of CH Diagnostics and Consulting in Fort Collins, Colorado, there is no danger to a dog from lapping up spring water or trail puddles. He says that almost every dog he has ever examined has giardiasis, which causes a soft stool only when the dog is first infected.

Do not turn your dog loose to enjoy a whopping run in strange farm country. Rural police usually have the authority to shoot an unchained dog on sight. As a simple courtesy to others in the camp area or on the trail, carry a small garden shovel to bury the dog's feces. Always have on hand a dog muzzle, garden shovel, metal leash, and the nearest vet's phone number.

Many American Red Cross chapters offer both a book and classes on pet first aid. Call your local chapter for information. There are two excellent books for suggested reading: *On the Trail with Your Canine Companion* by Cheryl Smith and *Hiking with Your Dog* by Gary Hoffman.

Helping Out in the Outdoors

Noble be man, helpful and good!
For that alone sets him apart
From every other creature on earth.

—Johann Wolfgang von Goethe (1749–1832)

For the retired seniors who have a love of the outdoors, there is no problem in finding specific places where you can put your hands to work at maintaining and improving America's wilderness. It's been around for years as a service of the American Hiking Society—an annual publication appropriately titled *Helping Out in the Outdoors*. It is a directory of internships and volunteer positions on the nation's public lands in every state. To find one that appeals to you, the AHS recommends the following guidelines:

1. Decide first in which state or region you want to work, what kind of work you'd like to do and whether you'll be working in a park, forest, or other land agency.
2. Contact the agency listed in the directory, and, says the AHS, ask questions: What kind of weather can you expect? What personal equipment should you bring? Will you be reimbursed for expenses? Will you have to pay for food? How long will the assignment last?

Here are some of the jobs available:

1. **Campground hosts**—They usually are required to work for extended periods of time. Their most important job is helping visitors get settled and suggesting things for them to do. They also help keep campgrounds neat and may perform light maintenance jobs. In return, hosts have a free campsite for the length of their job. Hosts usually provide their own trailer, camp facilities, or RV unit. Because the heaviest workload is on weekends, hosts often have free time during the week to explore and enjoy the area.
2. **Trail maintenance and trail crew**—These volunteers work hard. They clear brush, haul out stumps, repair erosion damage, and keep trails open. Volunteers use hand tools, such as picks and shovels, pulaskis, and saws. Some jobs involve packing in equipment on stock animals.

3. **Wilderness rangers and backcountry guards**—They will spend summers in some of the nation's most beautiful country, hiking trails by day and camping out at night. These workers often are alone for days at a time. The job often requires rangers to hike 10 to 20 miles a day while backpacking heavy loads. Much work involves contact with visitors and informing them about wilderness regulations. They also clear and maintain trails. Most assignments require rangers and guards to provide their own equipment.

4. **Club work**—Many American Hiking Society (AHS) clubs offer a variety of volunteer opportunities, which are listed in the directory. An indication of how extensive job possibilities, which include anything from spending a week helping clear a new path to spending a summer on a vigorous wilderness job, is that more than 500 are listed in the directory. Those interested should call the AHS at 301-565-6704, or www.americanhiking.org.

The AHS also runs a series of one-week outdoor "volunteer vacations." These are especially suitable for seniors. The cost, which includes everything from food to shelter, in 2002 was $80 a week. For information, call the AHS and ask for the booklet, *Volunteer Vacations*.

AFTERWORD

Setting out on the voyage to Ithaca
You must pray that the way be long,
Full of adventure and experiences.

—Constantine Cavafy (1863-1933)

The joy of a dynamic life—exploring fresh ideas, hiking unexplored trails—is not restricted by gender or age. It always awaits. To those who choose it, life is never-ending excitement.

Are you ever too old to pitch a tent in a wilderness? Or too old to read again the tome that first opened new worlds to you? Or too old to challenge, in thought or soul, tomorrow? At any age?

If years hamper the body, they do not hamper the spirit. Live abundantly!

You can. You will. There is no one to do it your way except you.

Without coercion your eyes scanned these pages, vibrant evidence that your dreams and hopes are alive, well, and seeking nourishment.